Living Your Faith

Closing the Gap Between Mind and Heart

Living Your Faith

Closing the Gap Between Mind and Heart

Terry L. Miethe

COLLEGE PRESS
PUBLISHING COMPANY
Joplin, Missouri

Copyright © 1993. College Press Publishing Co.

Unless otherwise noted, all Bible quotations are from the New American Standard Bible, © The Lockman Foundation, 1960, 1962, 1963, 1968, 1971, 1973, 1975, 1977.

Printed in the United States of America.

Library of Congress Catalog Card Number 93-73258
International Standard Book Number 0-89900-620-5

Dedication

"If all the world were Christian, it might not matter if all the world were educated. But, as it is, a cultural life will exist outside the Church whether it exists inside or not. To be ignorant and simple now — not to be able to meet the enemies on their own ground — would be to throw down our weapons, and to betray our uneducated brethren who have, under God, no defense but us against the intellectual attacks of the heathen. Good philosophy must exist, if for no other reason, because bad philosophy needs to be answered."
—C. S. Lewis, *The Weight of Glory and Other Addresses*, p. 50.

"Members of several churches proclaim that 'of course C.S. Lewis was one of us.' In fact C.S. Lewis was a Christian not given to 'isms,' and whilst he preferred to attend the local Anglican church, this was more a matter of convenience than of conviction. It was from him that I learnt that *Sectarianism is one of the Devil's keenest weapons against Christendom* [emphasis added].
—Douglas H. Gresham, *Lenten Lands: My Childhood with Joy Davidman and C.S. Lewis*, p. x.

This book is dedicated to the memory of C. S. Lewis; and to the hundreds — yes, thousands — of young Christians I pray God will raise up who must be willing to pay the price to use their minds in defense of the faith, as Lewis did, and who will work to make the seventeenth chapter of the Gospel of John a reality. These young Christians must be dedicated to the biblical vision of Christian unity. Lewis understood, as have many before him, that division in Christ's Church "is a horrid evil, fraught with many evils. It is anti-Christian, as it destroys the visible unity of the Body of Christ; as if he were divided against himself, excluding and ex-communicating a part of himself."

Before these young Christians can truly appreciate the genius of C. S. Lewis, let alone inherit his mantel, they will have to understand that such division or "sectarianism" is an evil of Satan himself! I pray, in the words of Jesus in John 17, and with the vision of Christian unity, that a whole generation of young Christians will see the evil and live to root it out of the church!

Other Works By Terry L. Miethe

The Metaphysics of Leonard James Eslick: His Philosophy of God, 1976.
Why Believe? God Exists! Rethinking the Case for God and Christianity, with Gary R. Habermas, 1993.
Does God Exist? A Believer and an Atheist Debate, with Antony G.N. Flew, 1991.
"The Universal Power of the Atonement," chapter four in *The Grace of God, The Will of Man*, 1989.
The Compact Dictionary of Doctrinal Words, 1988.
A Christian's Guide to Faith & Reason, 1987.
Did Jesus Rise from the Dead? The Resurrection Debate, with Gary R. Habermas and Antony G. N. Flew, 1987; paperback edition 1989.
The Philosophy and Ethics of Alexander Campbell: From the Context of American Religious Thought, 1800 to 1866, 1984.
The New Christian's Guide to Following Jesus, 1984.
Augustinian Bibliography, 1970-1980: With Essays on the Fundamentals of Augustinian Scholarship, 1982.
"Atheism: Nietzsche," chapter six in *Biblical Errancy: An Analysis of its Philosophical Roots*, 1981.
Thomistic Bibliography, 1940-1978, with Vernon J. Bourke, 1980.
Reflections, Vol. I, 1980; Vol. II, 1983; Vol. III, 1988; Vol. IV, 1988.

About the Author

TERRY L. MIETHE is Provost and Honored Professor of Philosophy, Theology, and History at Emmanuel College, Oxford. He is currently a postdoctoral fellow in history at Christ Church, the University of Oxford, England. Dr. Miethe holds the A.B., with honors, from Lincoln Christian College; the M.A., with honors, from Trinity Evangelical Divinity School; the M.Div. from McCormick Theological Seminary; the Ph.D. in Philosophy (Phi Beta Kappa), from Saint Louis University; and the A.M. and Ph.D. in social ethics and theology from the University of Southern California. He is a member of eight scholastic honor societies in History, Psychology, Classical Languages, English, Philosophy, including Phi Beta Kappa and Alpha Sigma Nu. Dr. Miethe has written or edited fifteen books, including works on Augustine and Aquinas. Dr. Miethe's books have been translated into German, Spanish, Korean, and Russian. He has also written dozens of articles.

Table of Contents

Preface 11
Introduction 15
  1 What Is Faith, Really? 21
  2 Isn't It Enough to Just Believe? 33
  3 Free in Christ to Know. 41
  4 God's Image Shines in Us 49
  5 Building the Faith in Our World 61
  6 Free to Win Souls to Christ 66
  7 Free to Love the Unlovely 77
  8 The Holy Spirit and Knowledge. 85
  9 Renewing the Mind: Key to Christian Living 93
  10 "Agony": Key to Christian Victory. 99
  11 Beware of "One-eyed" Kings 109
  12 The Disciplined Christian 119
Appendices:
  A. A View of Faith and Learning 133
  B. The Christian and Debate 137
  C. The Limits of Science. 143
  D. A Plea for the Practical Application of Christian
     Philosophy. 158
Select Bibliography 171

Preface

My life is committed to learning as much about Ultimate Reality as is possible and sharing this in meaningful ways with as many people as possible.
—*Reflections,* Vol. I

This book is about the Christian's need to know. Christianity, of all religions, has always claimed a unique relationship to the world of fact and knowledge. This relationship has the most serious implications for the way we live our personal lives and to our view of how "faith" and "reason" go together. In the Bible, truth is always the opposite of error, and certainly the Bible claims to be giving us truth. Jesus said, in John 8:31-32, "If you hold to my teaching, you are really my disciples. Then you will know the truth, and the truth will set you free" (NIV).

The great Christian doctrines are not just claims of important moral teaching, but are inseparably tied to actual historical facts, that is, *actual historical events*. When the Bible teaches that individual human beings must be born again (John 3:3ff.), this is only possible because Jesus was "born again" in an actual, physical, bodily resurrection (Matt. 28:17; 1 Cor. 15) at a specific time on a specific day in history. In the Corinthian passage (NIV), we should "stand firm" and we should, "always give [ourselves] fully to the work of the Lord, because you know that your labor in the Lord is not in vain" because of the historical fact of Jesus' resurrection.

It is my belief that the biblical doctrine of faith is the most central, foundational doctrine of all Christianity, and yet the most misunderstood. Because the relationship of "faith" and "reason" is so misunderstood, you find many Christians on one or two extreme — and biblically unacceptable — poles:

(1) Some think that Christianity is purely "rational"; (2) some think, and act as if Christianity is purely emotional or mystical. *Both are wrong!* G. K. Chesterton was certainly correct when he said, "The thing from which the world suffers just now more than from any other evil is not the assertion of falsehood, but the endless and irrepressible repetition of half-truths."

People who take the purely rational approach often think that it does not matter what they *do* or how they *feel*; it only matters what they *believe* about Christianity. These people tend to be conservative Christians who have fallen into the trap of "dead orthodoxy." They may believe and hold to all the "right" doctrines, but their lives are often exemplified by rigid legalism. They do not seem to be aware of the depth of Christian love and their own sinfulness. They are always expressing "righteous indignation" about something or someone, condemning rather than standing for what is morally right and showing the love and acceptance of Christ for the sinner — or they are fighting with other Christians.

People who take the purely emotional or mystical approach are often found in either liberal or conservative theological camps. The difference being that the conservative at least gives lip service to the historical, factual basis for Christianity while not realizing its importance in what actually constitutes "faith." Usually, too, they are unaware of their obligation to grow in knowledge in order to mature in their own Christian lives, which opens the way to effective, meaningful evangelism. To the liberal, the historical basis or truth of the Christian faith is not something one can prove. This is a matter of *personal* faith, What matters is how one treats his fellowman. This position *may* end up as nothing but humanism masked as Christianity, rendering individuals powerless to live the very ethic they claim.

Unfortunately, there are incredible numbers of conservative Christians who also suffer from this overly personalized faith. They, as has been noted, remain "true" doctrinally, but fall into a kind of Christian mysticism. God must be constantly "popping" minor or major miracles every day of their life for them to be happy. God becomes little more than a "celestial bellhop," taking care of selfish needs. One form of this mistake has manifested itself in a very dangerous cult, invading much of American Christianity, sometimes referred to as the "Gospel of Health and Wealth." These people believe — and it can be taught very subtly — that if God does not keep you healthy or make you wealthy, in a material sense, then there is something wrong with your faith.

In light of these extreme positions, it is time for a book that discusses the relationship of Christianity and knowledge, or the relationship of faith and reason. This relationship is most important to understanding essential Christianity and to Christian living and witnessing.

A word is appropriate here as to how this book came into being. This volume is really a product of my pilgrimage in faith, the result of 30 years of growing as a Christian, 24 years of ministry in local churches, and 21 years of teaching in colleges and universities. And it is the result of an innocent, but oft-asked question that was once put to me.

One day, when I was teaching part time at a small Christian college, I walked up to the desk of the college secretary and we began to talk about things in general, Out of the blue, knowing that I was working on a Ph.D. in philosophy, she asked, "Why would any Christian be interested in philosophy?"

I realized, by the way the question was posed, that this fline Christian woman — in regard to the relationship of faith and reason and the importance of knowledge to the Christian — suffered from the proverbial "blind spot," just like the actual blind spot in your car's rearview mirror. I knew that I had a double problem. Before I could really answer her question, I had to first reveal the presence of the blind spot, which would involve a lengthy discussion of the relationship of faith and reason. I set out to do this by writing, in the most elementary way I could, a five-part series of articles on the subject. These five articles, plus the years of teaching since, serve as the basis for this book.

It is my hope — my prayer — that at the end of this book, you understand the essential relationship between faith and reason, are inspired to want to know more, and become committed to use more the greatest gift our God has given you — the ability to think and to love (they are really inseparable and both are rooted in the mind) — to glorify our Lord and Savior, Jesus.

— Terry L. Miethe
30 May 1993
Pentecost (the celebration of the Birth of Christ's Church)
Oxford, England

Introduction

In the *Preface*, I said that *Living Your Faith* is about the Christian's need to know. It is. But it is about more than that really. It is about "Why your mind is important for faith." It is about *why* the Christian needs to know, *what* he is to know, and *how* to apply that knowledge in service to God and in Christian living. *Living Your Faith* affirms that faith and reason are not enemies, that they walk hand-in-hand, are inseparable really. Many Christians are troubled by the sense of there being a "missing link," a gap, between faith and their reasoning abilities. Shrinking back when confronted by skeptics and faltering when faced by their own doubts, many in the church need to know how to close the gap between mind and heart.

This book also tries to relate this need for an intelligent faith to the very practical aspects of Christian living, evangelism, victory over sin, what it really means to be created in God's image, Christian discipline and other important implications of living for Christ. If you read, and apply, what *Living Your Faith* teaches, you will have a new excitement about your Christian beliefs, escape from murky emotionalism, have a growing freedom from doubt, fresh hope and assurance in the gospel, and a greater boldness in sharing your faith. In short, you will have solid footing in a world riddled with shifting, ever-changing philosophies as you develop and understand a true Christian philosophy of life, or world view.

Chapter One treats "What Is Faith, Really?" It starts with the reflection that "Faith is a conscious mental desire to do the will of the God of Scripture!" Faith in the New Testament is not blindness, ignorance, or simple-mindedness. *A Christian's true vocation is being a Christian.* We should be practicing this every minute of our lives. Christian faith is trusting a living person, Jesus — trusting in His resurrection and in the Scripture. John Stott explains faith as "a reasoning trust." Chapter One recounts what many famous Christian scholars have said about faith and its relation to knowledge. It asserts that we who are Christians are supposed to always be ready to explain why we believe, to give an account for the hope that is in us.

Chapter two discusses the question: "Isn't It Enough to Just Believe?" It answers the questions: (1) "What Is Philosophy?" It affirms that the Christian philosopher has a rich tradition and important history. (2) "What Is Knowledge?" A Christian must know both content and also how to apply it to living. (3) "What Is Wisdom?" The Christian must be wise in living in this world. And (4) "Why Are These Important?" We see clearly that for the Christian believing is not some vacuous "believing on believing," or "faith in faith," but is based on evidence and the claims of historical fact.

Chapter three tells us we are "Free in Christ to Know." "As Christians, we simply cannot afford the luxury of ignorance." The very concept of being a *disciple* of Christ involves serious learning. Our whole lives must be shaped by our knowledge of Christ through His Word. Knowledge also brings us freedom in Christ. In the process of knowing His Word, and how it applies to this world, we are transformed so that we may prove God's will in our lives. It is only through knowing Christ and his Word that we can really love our fellow human beings.

Chapter four is a discussion of the important implications of the fact that "God's Image Shines in Us." What does it mean to be created in God's image? Why is the Bible so important to us as Christians? This chapter explains that deception is a mental act and that knowledge can help us control doubt. We see that knowledge is essential to Christian maturity.

Chapter five affirms that "Building the Faith in Our World" is our duty and privilege as Christians. Knowledge is necessary to confirm faith in believers. It is also essential in communicating faith to unbelievers. And, knowledge is very

INTRODUCTION

important in defending the faith to unbelievers. Every Christian is called to live the Christian life, to build the faith and to defend it (1 Peter 3:15).

Chapter six explains that we are "Free to Win Souls to Christ" and further relates the Christian's need to know to lifestyle evangelism. It asserts that evangelism is intelligent and discusses the example of the Apostle Paul. Argument can lead to conversion. Finally, it talks about the ideal versus the practical in regard to the Christian's need to know and evangelism.

Chapter seven makes it clear that we are "Free to Love the Unlovely." If the mark of a human being is the ability to reason, then inseparably related is the ability to love. This chapter explains that Christian love is far more than "humanistic" love. Christian love must, will, be expressed in service to God and to our fellow man. Christian love, like knowledge, comes from God. Christian love genuinely wills the best for another even if it is not the best for you. We see that the New Testament tells us much about God's love for us and about the characteristics of Christian love.

Chapter eight is a discussion of "The Holy Spirit and Knowledge." This chapter looks first at what the Scripture says about the Holy Spirit. Then, the fact that the Holy Spirit works in the lives of men is affirmed. And, finally the relationship of the Holy Spirit, the Scripture, and knowledge is treated. While being very concerned not to put God in a box, we must also understand that what is viewed as the action of the Holy Spirit cannot contradict what the Bible teaches. What we view as the work of the Holy Spirit must be judged according to the clear teaching of the Scripture. We want to be careful not to make Him less than He is and also be careful not to limit the power of the Holy Spirit.

Chapter nine looks in depth at Philippians 4:4-9 as teaching: "Renewing the Mind: Key to Christian Living." We are to rejoice in the Lord always. We are to let our forbearing spirit be known to all men. Rather than being anxious, we are to pray. Paul in this Scripture doesn't give us some "pie in the sky" philosophy but gives us the key to Christian living. He tells us that our minds must be properly disciplined and he tells us what we should think about to have victory in Christian living.

Chapter ten is entitled: "'Agony': Key to Christian Victory." This chapter tells us what "agony" really is: what Jesus experienced in the garden of Gethsemane. We see and understand that with His power, Jesus' "agony" is an example for Christians. We learn just how powerful Satan is. We see how we, as Christians, can defeat evil. Here we understand why prayer is so very important to the Christian. We also learn about a very essential requirement for victory in Christian living.

Chapter eleven warns us to "Beware of 'One-eyed' Kings!" The title comes from the old French saying: "In the country of the blind, the one-eyed men are kings." It discusses the problem with the church today and draws on an obscure figure in church history, Alcuin, as an example for us today. Who should be our authority in the faith? This chapter tells us that "education" is only part of the answer. The real emphasis is not the problem of the "One-eyed Kings," but the priesthood of all believers. This is the real answer to the problem of the church today.

Chapter twelve is a challenge to us all to be "The Disciplined Christian." We must be a real part of the solution, not just a part of the problem. We are first to seek the Kingdom of God *and* His righteousness. In doing this, diligence is vital to what must be a lifelong process. Chapter twelve ends with a challenge for the church, a prayer for you, and a "Postscript," by way of a warning. There will be a price to pay for learning to know God and for desiring to serve Him. Even knowledge of the truth is dangerous.

Following the twelve chapters, there are four appendices: *Appendix A* discusses "A View of Faith and Learning." It is a short treatment of the need, and method, of integration of an individual's personal faith and education. *Appendix B* looks at "The Christian and Debate." Is debating valuable for the Christian today? If a Christian does debate, of what should he be sure? *Appendix C* is a longer discussion of "The Limits of Science." Related to the whole area of faith and reason today is the question of whether believing is somehow contradictory

INTRODUCTION

to the evidence of modern science. *Appendix D* is an excellent discussion by my friend and brother Gary R. Habermas, regarding "A Plea for the Practical Application of Christian Philosophy." Dr. Habermas explains that the discipline of the mind, philosophy, has very practical implications for the Christian and is an important discipline for Christians if properly taught.

Each chapter, except chapter ten, begins with a reflection from one of my four volumes of *Reflections*. These are short attempts to get Christians to think about the simple truth of certain Christian principles. It is hoped that these *Reflections* might help Christians to spend some time in thought about their lives, their faith, and their commitment.

At the very end of the book is a "Select Bibliography." Now that you have been challenged to know what you believe and why, you will need resources for further study. The bibliography represents books covering the entire spectrum, from books for the beginner to those for the most advanced. You will not agree with everything in every book. You are not supposed to. As *Living Your Faith* has explained, you must use your mind to test the claims in the market place, and most importantly to *know* why you believe what you believe so that *you* can once again take the Christian faith into the world where it so desperately needs to be!

1 What Is Faith, Really?

Faith is a conscious mental desire to do the will of the God of Scripture!
—*Reflections,* Vol. I

The twentieth century is perhaps the greatest period of educational advance in the history of civilization. From the time of the ancient Greeks, men have dreamed of soaring in the heavens. At Kitty Hawk, North Carolina, in 1903, Wilbur and Orville Wright made the first successful powered flight. Just sixty-six years later, man fulfilled centuries of dreams by landing on the moon. For the past hundred years, science and scientists have controlled most human progress. Scientism has led many to give up their faith in God. But we must understand the limits of science. (For a further discussion of this topic, see Appendix C.)

A famous theologian, Rudolph Bultmann, said this of the conflict between faith and science: "The scientific world picture is here to stay and will assert its right against any theology, however imposing, that conflicts with it." Very interestingly, the particular "scientific world picture" that this theologian accepted as absolute is no longer in vogue in science. Bultmann also said:

> The idea of wonder as miracle has become almost impossible for us today because we understand the processes of nature as governed by law . . . the idea of miracle has, therefore, become untenable and must be abandoned.[1]

---

[1]Rudolf Bultmann, *Kerygma and Myth,* edited by Hans Werner Bartsch (New York: Harper & Row, 1961), especially "New Testament and Mythology," pp. 1-44.

But as Christians have realized for centuries, the "idea of... miracle" and "the processes of nature as governed by law" do not conflict. In fact, the idea that nature acts uniformly, which is essential to modern science, is also essential to the Christian view of miracle. For the Christian, nature's uniformity was born out of and can only be trusted if a Christian metaphysic is true, i.e., that there is a Supreme Mind and Personality behind nature.[2]

Many have insisted, however, that loyalty to the modern scientific view cannot be sacrificed, and that one's concept of the Christian faith must be revised in light of science. Scientific knowledge has advanced greatly, even in the "common man," while biblical knowledge seems to have seriously declined even (one might say especially) in the churches. Does this mean that biblical faith has also declined? To answer this question one must ask, "What is faith, really?" What does the Bible say faith is?

Faith and the Church

What exactly is faith as presented in the New Testament? We will see. It certainly is not blindness, ignorance, or simple-mindedness. It seems that many in the church think it all right to be educated in areas relating to their vocations. When it comes to their faith, they think it only necessary to believe the elementary doctrines. They think that to question why they believe or what they believe is to be disrespectful to God. We forget that for a Christian, his vocation *is* Christ. His chief responsibility is to serve God with his total being. Jesus said the greatest commandment, for us all, is, "You shall love the Lord your God with all your heart, and with all your soul, and with all your mind" (Matt. 22:37). Oliver R. Barclay quotes this passage from Mark 12:30, which adds "and with all your strength." Then Barclay writes:

> Having a Christian mind is therefore no small thing. It is part of the first and greatest commandment... and it comes

---

[2]C. S. Lewis, *Miracles: A Preliminary Study* (New York: Macmillan, 1947), pp. 108-109.

in a place in the whole scheme of Christian salvation which makes it crucial to both Christian conduct and Christian character as well as to Christian thought. . . .This needs emphasis at the present time, because the current culture of the Western world is tending to put feelings so much before thinking that it has in some circles become hard to defend Christian thinking at all.[3]

Therefore, a Christian's *avocation* is that which he does to earn a living. His true *vocation* is learning about, and service to God. One might think from observing many Sunday schools — the lessons presented in them and the way we prepare for these lessons — that we in the church are unconcerned about Christians being educated in the faith, and that we are apparently against biblical/theological education altogether. In fact, it is not just the Sunday schools that give us this impression. Look at the preaching in many, many churches. It is very common to hear it said, as a proud slogan, "We preach only the Bible." But there is a very great difference between preaching *about* the Bible and preaching *from* the Bible.

Preaching *about* the Bible occurs when a preacher opens his Bible, reads a text, and leaves it open as a prop — and then talks for thirty or forty minutes using popular stories or illustrations. Preaching *from* the Bible occurs when the preacher tells us what the Bible says, why it says it, and how it applies to our lives at home, at work, at play. In other words, biblical preaching is expository, exegetical preaching. There is certainly a place for textual, topical preaching, but you cannot mature Christians with a steady diet of stories and illustrations.

Again, we have heard so often, "We must preach the whole counsel of God" meaning we must preach all that He has commanded us (Matt. 28:20). But preaching the whole counsel of God is so very different than the kind that never does, in fact, give people the biblical meat necessary to mature in their understanding of Christian commitment. Preachers *must* see the relationship between faith and reason and must be willing to spend long hours in biblical study.

---

[3]Oliver R. Barclay, *The Intellect and Beyond* (Grand Rapids, MI: Zondervan, 1985), pp. 10-11.

Even if we are not willing to admit it, we seem to agree with H. L. Mencken that "faith may be defined briefly as an illogical belief in the occurrence of the improbable." Paul Little used to tell the story of the Sunday school teacher who asked the class, "What is faith?" To this question a young boy quickly answered, "Believing something you know isn't true." Certainly this is not what we find faith to be as revealed in the New Testament. Little has written:

> It is not enough to know *what* we believe. It is essential to know *why* we believe it. Believing something doesn't make it true. A thing is true or not regardless of whether anyone believes it.[4]

We who claim to be Christians *must* know why we believe what we believe, especially in today's age of scientism.

Faith and Practice

I once heard a radio commentator say, "If you don't practice it, you don't believe it." Can we then say that if you do not practice the Christian faith, you do not have faith?

James tells us that the demons were the original "faith only" Protestants. He says that people who "want evidence that faith without deeds is useless" are foolish (v. 20). If there is anything we must stop in our churches it is "easy believism." James also tells us that those who only listen, Sunday after Sunday, to the word are deceiving themselves. We must: "Do [practice] what it says" (James 1:22-25). What *is* practicing the Christian faith?

The New Testament teaches that practicing the Christian faith always involves two aspects for every Christian: the worship of God and teaching — teaching someone to bring him to Christ, or teaching him to help him mature in Christ. Matt. 28:19-20, commonly called "The Great Commission," was intended for every Christian, not just ordained ministers. It tells us that Christians have a responsibility to "go and make disciples." Making disciples involves teaching and witnessing

---

[4]Paul E. Little, *Know Why You Believe* (Downers Grove, IL: InterVarsity, 1972), p. 1.

before and after the conversion of the individual. The fact is that Christians and churches are not taking their responsibility to disciple new converts seriously. Many times the back doors of our churches are far wider than the front!

Jesus said, "If you abide in My word, then you are truly disciples of Mine; and you shall know the truth, and the truth shall make you free" (John 8:31, 32). This is because Jesus is the Truth. Knowledge plays an important part in our being able to be free in Him. The biblical concept of faith seems to presuppose that we will develop the ability to defend our faith to anyone who asks (Acts 9:26-31; 17:2-4, 17, 22-34; 1 Pet. 3:15; and 2 Pet. 1:16-21). But how can we "defend," support and explain that which we do not really know?

Shortly after I started ministering to a church, I had a friend, a high school guidance counselor who had preaching experience, speak at a morning service. At the end, during prayer, he asked all those who knew the plan of salvation and could share it with another individual to raise their hands. Very few did. His point was that if you were not sure of the plan of salvation yourself and if you could not share it with others, how in the world were you ever going to be able to be an instrument of the Holy Spirit to bring someone to Christ let alone be able to disciple anyone?

Trust, and Its Basis

The word *faith* appears only 2 times in the Old Testament (Deut. 32:20 and Hab. 2:4). It appears 307 times in the New Testament. When you consult a Greek dictionary for definitions of faith, you will find two essential aspects that penetrate to the heart of the biblical teaching: (1) trust or acceptance; belief that Jesus is Lord, with acknowledgment of His resurrection, and (2) intellectual content, the revealed truth that is firmly believed, and is reflected in the life of the believer.

John Stott explains faith as "a reasoning trust, a trust which reckons thoughtfully and confidently upon the trustworthiness of God."[5] Faith, according to Josh McDowell, is

---

[5]John R. W. Stott, *Your Mind Matters: The Place of the Mind in the Christian Life* (Downers Grove, IL: InterVarsity, 1972), p. 36.

"the assurance of the heart [mind, the center of our consciousness] in the adequacy of the evidence.[6] This seems to reflect the significance of Heb. 11:1, which says: "Now faith is the substance of things hoped for, the evidence of things not seen" (KJV). The Greek word translated as evidence in the King James literally means "proof, proving."

The *New International Version* carries the weight of the text when it says: "Now faith is being sure of what we hope for and *certain of what we do not see*" (emphasis mine). Why do people read this passage and make faith something mystical, something blind? This interpretation is certainly not in the passage; in fact, just the opposite. Faith is the proof of things not seen by us, but definitely seen by others. There certainly was proof, evidence afforded for belief.

Richard Swinburne, in *Faith and Reason*, says:

> A major constituent of faith . . . is belief — that or *propositional belief*. The man who has faith in God . . . believes that there is a God and believes certain propositions about him. The faith which the Christian religion commends is *basically faith in a person or persons, God (or Christ)* characterized as possessing certain properties and having done certain actions; and secondarily perhaps in some of the deeds which he has done, and the good things which he has provided and promised. . . . It has been the opinion of the considerable majority of theologians down the centuries that Christian faith is voluntary. . . . That faith, *which is trust in God*, is voluntary.[7]

A basic *proposition* is that which seems to a man to be true, and therefore, he is inclined to believe it. It is forced upon him by his experience of the world, according to Swinburne:

> A basic proposition will acquire the status of a belief (and we may then call it a basic belief) unless other of a man's basic beliefs render it improbable . . . all beliefs give rise to action and must be based on evidence.[8]

---

[6]Josh McDowell, *Evidence that Demands a Verdict* (San Bernardino, CA: Campus Crusade for Christ, 1972), p. 4.
[7]Richard Swinburne, *Faith and Reason* (Oxford, England: Clarendon Press, 1981), pp. 3, 104, 124, 200.
[8]*Ibid.*, pp. 20-21, 33.

WHAT IS FAITH, REALLY?

We do not find "blind faith" anywhere in the New Testament. Even the trust or acceptance aspect of faith is not blind. Dr. Lloyd-Jones makes a very important statement in commenting on Matt. 6:30, in which Jesus chides His listeners for having "little faith":

> Faith according to our Lord's teaching in this paragraph, is primarily thinking; and the whole trouble with a man of little faith is that he does not think... his thought is being controlled by something else. . . .That is the essence of worry. . . .That is not thought; that is the absence of thought, a failure to think.[9]

God has given us more than enough evidence that we can trust. We are provided with historically reliable evidence that can be tested as any history can. Thank God for it!

Richard L. Purtill, in the first part of his book *Reason to Believe*, shows "that the Christian faith is not nonsensical and that none of the common arguments against it is successful." In the second part, Purtill says:

> Thus we showed that it is not unreasonable to believe in Christianity. Some Christians seem to feel that this is all reason can be expected to do in this area, and that then faith must take over. That this is not the biblical view nor the traditional Christian view is, I think, clear from a study of the scriptures and a study of history. It is also, I believe, based on a misunderstanding of the nature of faith. *Faith must be based on reasons, and the reasons must be good ones* [emphasis added].[10]

Purtill thinks that C. S. Lewis' formula is the best when Lewis says that faith is ". . . assent to a proposition which we think so overwhelmingly probable that there is a psychological exclusion of doubt although not a logical exclusion of dispute."[11] Our faith based on the very good reasons, or evidence, Purtill says are necessary for it — can reach a level

---

[9] D. Martyn Lloyd-Jones, *Studies in the Sermon on the Mount*, vol. 2 (Grand Rapids, MI: Eerdmans, 1970), pp. 129-130.
[10] Richard L. Purtill, *Reason to Believe* (Grand Rapids, MI: Eerdmans, 1974), pp. 71- 75.
[11] C. S. Lewis, "On Obstinacy in Belief" in *The World's Last Night and Other Essays* (New York: Brace Jovanovich, 1955), p. 16.

where we are so sure of the evidence that there is a "psychological exclusion of doubt," but we must be willing throughout life to constantly examine, or reexamine the evidence.

The Object of Faith

It does not matter how *much* faith we have. What matters is the object in which we have our faith. John Warwick Montgomery, in the *Shape of the Past*, says, "If our Christ of faith deviates at all from the Biblical Jesus of history, then to the extent of that deviation, we also lose the genuine Christ of faith,"[12] While reasserting this in his later book, *Faith Founded on Fact*, by saying, "In the deepest sense, the Bible identifies truth with the person of Jesus Christ, the God-man who came to earth to die for the sins of the world" (John 14:6). Montgomery also relates that evidence of this truth is necessary and that Jesus himself and Paul were willing to give such evidence (e.g., Thomas in John 20:24-29, Paul's Areopagus address in Acts 17).[13]

Montgomery goes on to ask:

> What is the non-Christian to do, when amid this din he hears the Christian message? Are we Christians so naive as to think that he will automatically, *ex opere operato*, accept Christianity as true and put away world-views contradicting it? And if we call out to him, "Just try Christianity and you will find that it proves itself experientially," do we really think that he will not at the same time hear precisely the same subjective-pragmatic appeal from numerous other quarters?[14]

The answer to the question is clear, historically and scripturally. Montgomery is right when he asserts that for an effective Christian witness in a pluralistic world, we need "an objective apologetic — a 'reason for the hope that is in you' — that will give the non-Christian clear ground for experientially

---

[12]John Warwick Montgomery, *The Shape of the Past: An Introduction to Philosophical Historiography* (Ann Arbor, MI: Edwards Brothers, 1962), p. 145. Now published by Bethany House Publishers.

[13]John Warwick Montgomery, *Faith Founded on Fact: Essays in Evidential Apologetics* (Nashville, TN: Thomas Nelson, 1978), pp. 35-38.

[14]*Ibid.*, pp. 39-42.

trying the Christian faith."

> Absolute proof of the truth of Christ's claims is available only in personal relationship with Him; but contemporary man has every right to expect us to offer solid reasons for making such a total commitment. The apologetic task is justified not as a rational substitute for faith, but as a ground for faith; not as a replacement for the Spirit's working, but as a means by which the objective truth of God's Word can be made clear so that men will heed it as the vehicle of the Spirit who convicts the world through its message.[15]

Saving faith literally means to "believe into." It denotes a faith which takes a man out of himself and puts him into Christ. This kind of faith carries an intellectual assent that ties itself with the strongest possible bonds to Jesus. It is trusting a person — Jesus, the Christ. Thus the two aspects of faith make it not a passing thing, but a continuing attitude of life. Christian faith is not a way of life, it is life. If we are not living as Christians, we are only existing. In the Greek *pistis* (faith) we have the first turning to "trust" and "acceptance." In *gnosis* (knowledge) we have that continual growth in knowledge to which faith advances. One can say that faith is a conscious mental desire to do the will of the God of the Bible.

Present Your Case

In the words of Isa. 41:21, God issues a great challenge to false gods: " 'Present your case,' the Lord says. 'Bring forward your strong arguments,' the King of Jacob says." Clark Pinnock, in *Set Forth Your Case*, writes:

> Certainly the Lord himself does not shrink from the demand for authenticating credentials on the part of the gospel. Our good news is an accredited claim and bona fide offer. Our confidence in its objective truth is reflected in our zeal for its defense and proclamation.[16]

And if God does not shrink from the demand for proof why

---

[15]*Ibid.*, p. 42.
[16]Clark Pinnock, *Set Forth Your Case* (Chicago, IL: Moody Press, 1967), p. 7.

should we? What is faith, really? Probably the best answer can be found in 1 Pet. 3:15: "But sanctify Christ as Lord in your hearts, always being ready to make a defense to every one who asks you to give an account for the hope [faith] that is in you, yet with gentleness and reverence." The apostles called men to an intelligent faith in Jesus because He was and is God! And all of us who claim the name of Christ today should do the same because we also are commanded to be ready at all times.

You may ask, "Doesn't the Bible tell us to become like little children? (Matt. 18:3). Doesn't a small child come with 'blind faith' or a lack of knowledge? If you hold out your hands and tell your child who is sitting on a countertop to jump, he will jump. Isn't that an example of faith on the part of your child?"

The senior minister of the church in which I was an associate minister tells a story of exactly that happening with his youngest son. The son was sitting on the fender of a car and the father was playing with him, The father reached out his hands and called to the child to jump. But this particular time, just as the father called 'jump," the mother, who was some distance away called to the father and distracted him so that he looked away. And in that instant, the son jumped and fell to the ground. Though the child was not seriously hurt, the senior minister readily admitted that it was quite a while before his son would jump again when he held out his hands.

You see, a closer examination of the case in point does not support the idea that the child responds with "blind" faith. Rather the faith that makes the child willing to jump is based on the child's intimate knowledge of his parents. The child *knows* that he can trust his father to catch him because he has experienced his father's care and love. That trust is shaken for a time after the child falls to the ground. It takes some time before that knowledge of trust can be restored. This, in fact, turns out to be a good example of biblical faith because the trust or assurance is based on intimate knowledge both intellectual and emotional.

Certainly it is the same when a small child accepts Christ as Savior. I am not personally in favor of *trying* to get small children to "be saved," but when it happens you can bet that that child has been *taught* to pray from a very early age and has been *taught* much about God formally and informally by his parents. Again, it is certainly not an example of "blind" faith; in fact, on closer examination we see it is just the opposite.

Now, let us proceed throughout the rest of the book to answer the question: "How does this understanding of faith relate to who we are and what we do with our lives?"

2 Isn't It Enough to Just Believe?

There is no such thing as an ignorant question. There are only uninformed questioners. And the best way to remain so is not to ask questions.

Reflections, Vol. II

Unfortunately, many Christians today seem to feel that knowledge, either secular or biblical, general or specific, is not very important. Certainly knowledge, whatever its content, is not as important as believing, or having faith, they say. As a professor and student of philosophy and theology, I have been asked many times, "Why should a Christian be interested in philosophy?" In other words, what does reason have to do with revelation or knowing with believing?

To be sure, this question has been asked throughout the history of the church. The great men of the faith recognized both the importance of the question and the fact that knowing and believing must not be separated. Men like the Apostle Paul, Augustine of Hippo, Anselm of Canterbury, Thomas Aquinas, Martin Luther, John Calvin, John Wesley and Alexander Campbell have formulated answers to this question.

Yet great numbers of contemporary Christians still do not understand either the importance of the question or the essential relationship of faith and reason. Every semester in my introduction to philosophy class, students are strengthened in their understanding of Christianity and their commitment to Christ when they begin to realize the answer. But the battle is not won there, for these students come from churches and homes that also do not understand this essential relationship.

The following is part of a letter written by a former student:

What is it that causes people to be so afraid of stretching their mind? Why is it that the mere mention of the word "philosophy" causes people to be wary, and even more, steel themselves against the discussion of it by activating all mental defense mechanisms? What causes people to be so narrow-minded about such a broad-minded subject?*

Obviously, the answer to these questions is complex and depends on the particular experiences of individuals. Certainly many people have had a bad experience with "philosophy," perhaps in a "secular" university classroom. It is true, in my experience, that philosophy in that context is often used not to encourage faith, or even knowledge, but to make fun even of the possibility of knowing. (See Appendix B, "A Plea for the Practical Teaching of Philosophy.")

But on a basic level, I believe that many people fear education. And certainly education can be misused. I fear its opposite far more. After all, the only way to combat the misuse of education is to know (John 8:32).

Another reason people feel this way about philosophy, I am convinced, is that deep inside they realize they have such little knowledge of why they believe what they believe. So they are constantly afraid someone is going to win them over to unbelief with arguments or philosophy. And, of course, we have already mentioned other reasons. For instance, they have been told not to think or "question" because that is disrespectful to God. Or they have been told that Scripture is against knowledge. As we will soon see, none of these reasons are valid for a Christian. Still, before we can answer the question, "What does reason have to do with faith?" four preliminary questions must be discussed.

What Is Philosophy?

Philosophy has been called the most general science, the first principles of any intellectual discipline. At first, philosophy was thought of as the rational explanation of anything. Later it became known as the science of the first principles of being (i.e., metaphysics — the study of what it is to exist with-

---

*This letter is quoted with the permission of the student.

out any limitations, ultimately the philosophy of God); the presuppositions of ultimate reality. The discipline of philosophy is now divided into *metaphysics* (or ontology), *epistemology* (how we know what we know), *logic* (investigating the structure of propositions and of deductive reasoning), *ethics* (the study of systems of moral principles, right and wrong, good and bad, etc.), *aesthetics* (the qualities perceived in works of art, the idea of beauty), *philosophy of science, philosophy of religion, philosophy of history* (the study of foundational issues in these disciplines, and others).

Our English word philosophy comes from two Greek words: *philos* and *sophia*, which mean "love" and "wisdom." A philosopher, then, is one who is a lover of wisdom. A philosopher, by historical function and definition, is an honest searcher after truth wherever it may be found. Certainly this is also a chief characteristic of a Christian. Arthur Holmes, in *Philosophy: A Christian Perspective*, says:

> The popular concept of a "philosophy of life" or a "world view" makes sense in this context. It suggests a reflective outlook on life as a whole which gives meaning to the parts, ties our beliefs and values together, and provides a sense of direction amid life's innumerable paths.[1]

This sounds strangely reminiscent of Scripture: "How much better it is to get wisdom than gold! And to get understanding is to be chosen above silver" (Prov. 16:16; see also 2:6; 4:7). New Testament teaching is always equated with truth, and truth is always the opposite of error (Rom. 2:8).

Thomas Aquinas listed three very important ways philosophy can be of use to the Christian: (1) to establish logically those things which are preambles of faith, i.e., the existence of God, that He is one, etc.; (2) to help us understand by certain similitudes doctrines of the faith (Augustine used many likenesses from philosophy to explain the Trinity); and (3) to show that statements against the Christian faith are false or not necessarily true.[2]

---

[1]Arthur F. Holmes, *Philosophy: A Christian Perspective* (Downers Grove, IL: InterVarsity, 1975), p. 9.
[2]Vernon J. Bourke, *The Pocket Aquinas* (New York: Washington Square Press, 1960), p. 293.

The Christian philosopher thus has a rich tradition and important history. Christian philosophy can help the believer and the unbeliever to know the evidence for a Christian world view (reason one of Aquinas), to better understand the essence of the faith (reason two), to expose claims against the faith that are not true and to show — though all the evidence may not be in — that the Christian position is a credible intellectual position as against the counterclaims of its opponents (reason three). All of these are extremely important to the individual Christian and to the church. Christians, therefore, must be good philosophers.

What Is Knowledge?

Webster says knowledge is "the act, fact, or state of knowing; acquaintance with facts." This is foundational to the Christian in regard to both the Bible and philosophy, i.e., the Word and the world. In fact, the Bible itself presupposes that the believer needs knowledge both of the Word (God's special revelation, the Bible) and of the world. There are two words for knowledge in the Greek New Testament and they shed light on this, Before a person can teach anything, especially the Bible, he or she would have to know — both *ginosko*, which means comprehending knowledge, and *oida*, which means intimately knowing — what he or she is teaching. A Christian is required to know on the levels of both comprehension and intimacy.

Christian liberal arts colleges have long recognized the importance of liberal arts education, though Christian Bible colleges have not been willing to admit or have been slow to see this. (See Appendix A, "A View of Faith and Learning") This importance was emphasized by Woodrow Wilson, the only President of the United States who had an earned Ph.D. degree, as quoted in the *Phi Beta Kappa Handbook for New Members:*

> The educated man is to be discovered by his point of view, by the temper of his mind, by his attitude towards life and his fair way of thinking. He can see, he can discriminate, he can combine ideas and perceive whither they lead; he has insight and comprehension. His mind is a practised instrument of appreciation. He is more apt to contribute light than heat to a

discussion, and will oftener than another show the power of uniting the elements of a difficult subject in whole view; he has the knowledge of the world which no one can have who knows only his own generation or only his own task (quoted from *The Spirit of Learning,* 1909).

What educational attributes could possibly be more important to the mental and spiritual maturity of a Christian? Some Bible colleges are beginning to realize that liberal arts education is foundational to their students. Wilson went on to say:

What we should seek to impart in our colleges, therefore, is not so much learning itself as the spirit of learning. You can impart that to young men [and young women]; and you can impart it to them in the three or four years at your disposal. It consists in the power to distinguish good reasoning from bad, in the power to digest and interpret evidence.

Christians need to be taught systematically how to think through problems or circumstances, how to apply their knowledge of the Bible to everyday life situations. They need to learn to sort out accurate from inaccurate statements, reality from fantasy, factual statements from opinion, Gross generalities and the use of improper techniques of argument (e.g., "appeal to force," "abusing the opposition," "appeal to authority," "appeal to the masses," "appeal to pity," "argument from ignorance," "begging the question," "straw man arguments," etc.[3]) and other means of influencing human behavior by appealing to the emotions are much used in our society. Christians not only need to have a strong base in factual knowledge, but also the ability to point out what methods of argumentation are being abused. They need to be able to analyze problems, synthesize material, and deduce conclusions based on how the facts fit the situation.

This is essential to that endeavor we call "witnessing."

What Is Wisdom?

Wisdom is good judgment based on knowledge. If

---

[3]See a good introductory logic book on the informal fallacies, e.g., S. Morris Engel's *With Good Reason: An Introduction to Informal Fallacies* (New York; St. Martin's Press, 1982).

Christians have a need to know, certainly they have a responsibility to use that knowledge in good judgment. Alfred North Whitehead asserted, "Education is the acquisition of the art of the utilization of knowledge. This is an art very difficult to impart."[4] Certainly this is the "art" Christian colleges should be trying to impart in the context of both the Word and the world.

How can a Christian hold to a faith that he or she considers unreasonable? Faith is more than understanding. It is more than intellectual, but let it not be less. There are always moral considerations as a result of the intellectual truth of Christianity. Because Christian truth is more than a logical exercise, its content demands a way of life. This is why, as Holmes says, the biblical scholar engages in a study of the text to be sure of accurate transmission; in grammatical and historical exegesis in order to understand the writer's intent, in every literary science that helps toward a clear and correct understanding of divine revelation.[5] Biblical scholarship becomes all the more important because of the relevance of its truth to the everyday lives of men. The Christian is required to be wise in regard to both biblical and intellectual content.

Why Are These Important?

We are just coming out of a very strong anti-intellectual phase in society. Especially in our time, we must reject the idea that trying to justify faith in any way at all is lacking reverence for God. In fact, that idea is a basic misunderstanding of the biblical concept of faith. Faith is not an extra-mental process. It is acceptance based on intellectual content. "To say, as a Christian should, that only the faith which believes God on the basis of knowledge is true faith is to say something which causes an explosion in the twentieth-century world."[6]

---

[4]Alfred North Whitehead, *The Aims of Education* (New York: Macmillan, 1929), p. 16.
[5]Holmes, *Philosophy: A Christian Perspective*, p. 22.
[6]Francis A. Schaeffer, *The God Who is There* (Downers Grove, IL: InterVarsity, 1968), p. 142.

ISN'T IT ENOUGH TO JUST BELIEVE?

We must reject the idea that belief cannot argue with unbelief; it can only preach to it. This idea is completely futile. It is impossible to separate faith from reason. And when the Christian does so, all he accomplishes is to compromise the faith and destroy any possible basis for communicating with the unbeliever. It is dangerous to try to separate faith from reason. When you separate the two it lowers all defense against bigotry and fanaticism. Sincerity is not, nor has it ever been, a test for truth. Most people who are wrong are *sincerely* wrong.

The rejection of reason is really disguised pride ("I am right but I won't say why") or superego ("My thoughts are God's thoughts"). That is not the Christian faith I find in Scripture or history, nor is it a faith that will ever be satisfying to me or unbelievers.

Extremely bad things have happened historically whenever Christians have tried to separate faith from reason. How can you have a Christian world view if all you have is an individual opinion that is subjectively verifiable at best? How can you support your claims in relation to the great number of other religions claiming to have the truth, which also say they are personally, or subjectively verifiable? About all you can say to such claims is that mine is true for me. And they will say to you that theirs is true for them.

Why would the God who created the world and all that is in it, language, logic (the way God himself thinks) and so forth, then make belief in Him totally subjective and unknowable except to an individual person by way of a mystical experience? Of course, this contradicts the very notion and purpose of the Scripture.

May every Christian study God's Word and how it applies to the things of this world so that we might grow to maturity in Christ and bring others, with the help and work of the Holy Spirit, to the place where they might know Him.

3 Free in Christ to Know

As Christians, we simply cannot afford the luxury of ignorance.
—Reflections, Vol. I

Knowledge plays an important role in those doctrines of Christianity that are foundational to it, essential to the teachings of Jesus. Chief among these is the resurrection of Jesus, the supreme miracle and, if it is true, the fact of history. Without question Christianity, as a religion, is based on claims to truth, fact and knowledge — knowledge of God and of ultimate reality (truth in relation to this world and beyond), as created and sustained by God. In each of these doctrines, factual knowledge and historical evidence are important elements distinguishing biblical teaching and the claims of Christianity from other religions. If Christianity is true, it is because its great doctrines were actual historical events as reported by the apostles.

Either Christian faith is founded on fact — actual historical events — or it is not. If it is not, then certainly Christianity is not what it claims either in Scripture or in history. If Christianity is founded on fact, then these facts must be *knowable* in the same way other facts are knowable. Second Peter 1:16-18 says:

> For we did not follow *cleverly devised tales* when we made known to you the power and coming of our Lord Jesus Christ, but *we were eyewitnesses* of His majesty. For when He received honor and glory from God the Father, such an utterance as this was made to Him by the Majestic Glory, "This is My beloved Son with whom I am well-pleased" — and *we ourselves heard* this utterance made from heaven when we were with Him on the holy mountain [emphasis added].

The claim here is clearly that the information about Jesus related by the apostles was true, factual knowledge recorded by eyewitnesses. The information given us by the apostles, if true, is not of human invention, but is based on divine action and declaration — which they themselves saw and heard.

Robert Richardson, biographer and personal physician of Alexander Campbell, summarized Campbell's view of knowledge in relation to Christian faith: "No distinction between knowledge and faith . . . should . . . be permitted. They are distinguishable only by the sources from whence they are derived."[1] It was Mr. Campbell's position that reason had to decide if any testimony was true, and that if so decided, this was called believing. On the other hand, if reason decided the testimony was false, it resulted in disbelieving.

The Concept of Discipleship

The word *disciple* is based on the verb "to learn." It denotes a pupil, a learner, and especially with regard to the followers of Jesus, an adherent to the thing learned. Thus a disciple of Christ must, by definition, be a learner and a doer. It is obvious from the beginning that the doing must be based on the learning. How can we be doers if we have not first learned to know God and, through study of Scripture, His will for our lives?[2]

Disciple always implies a personal relationship which shapes the whole life of the one discipled. Christ, as no other teacher, embodied His teaching. The Christian is a disciple only when he adheres to Christ in both thought and action. There is a great difference between "decision making" and "disciple making," which the church today must learn. This is graphically illustrated by the following facts. When one of the largest churches in America held a week or two of "evangelism," there were 2400 decisions, 400 of these actually were

---

[1] Alexander Campbell, *The Millennial Harbinger* (1840), p. 460.
[2] See Paul E. Little, *Affirming the Will of God* (Downers Grove, Ill.; InterVarsity, 1971) and Carry Friesen, *Decision Making & The Will of God: A Biblical Alternative to the Traditional View* (Portland, OR: Multnomah Press, 1980).

baptized and became church members, but a year later only seven were active in the church. Of course we know what statistic was announced.*

How can we go about making disciples of those who have made a decision? May I suggest the following if the ministerial staff is serious about making disciples:

1. Preach from the New Testament *often*. This is how Christians are matured. So often, almost all I hear in some churches is preaching from the Old Testament where the preacher seems to feel that it is easy to pick out a good story and moralize about it for a half-hour to forty-five minutes. Of course this method of *using* — I should say "abusing" — the Old Testament can be quite convenient as it does not take much preparation time, but that is not how Christians are matured.

2. Study your passage, or lesson, carefully — exegetically — and use good commentaries. If you want to mature your people, either by way of a sermon or a lesson, then you need to be giving them the *meat* of the Word so that they know what it really says. It is not always clear — obviously — what a certain text actually says. And we certainly do not know what it says by pulling it out of context and just using it to illustrate what we want it to. *Why does* it says what it says? What was the message that the Holy Spirit wanted us to get from that verse or passage? And *how* does it apply to life at home, work, or play? Application is very important to a sermon or lesson. But all three of these elements have to be present if it is going to be biblical preaching or teaching.

3. Spend at least twenty hours a week minimum in sermon preparation. You cannot mature the people in the church if you have not done your homework. This can be a reality if the ministerial staff has trained a good support group in the church that is carrying on ministry, that is, sharing in the calling, evangelism, teaching, and even the preaching. Only when we take the priesthood of all believers seriously can the pastor/teacher be freed up to do the job Scripture says he

---

*I am not criticizing the church or its methods. I am making the point that we must take the responsibility of making disciples more seriously.

should do: preparing the saints for the work of ministry so that the body of Christ might be built up (Eph. 4:11-12).

4. Have at least a detailed outline, if not a manuscript, for your message or lesson. The manuscript should be 90 percent memorized, ten percent read. We must stop the "boxcar" approach to preaching — just one story or illustration after another. If we really respect the Bible as God's Word, then we will want to be very careful about what we say about what it means. Effective communication demands a well-thought-out presentation.

5. Teach your people to *want* and *expect* to be fed by feeding them consistently. Certainly any sermon or lesson should be clear, interesting, aimed at the heart (intended to motivate people to take action), as well as the mind (logical, and positive). You *cannot* mature the people if they are not taught.

A church will be about like our children. We will get out of them pretty much what we expect of them — not much more or less. I think the best way to judge the health and maturity of a church is not by the size of the attendance, or by the size of the offering, but by the number of members who are demanding to be disciples — taught regularly — so that they can go make disciples.

Knowledge Brings Freedom in Christ

It should be quite apparent to any Christian that the basic kind of knowledge needed by any man, indeed the very reason for the special revelation of Scripture, is knowledge of the truth. Christ is the Truth that enables men to be free (John 8:31, 32). More than intellectual recognition is involved in knowing the truth as Jesus means it, but certainly not less. Again this is comprehensive and intimate knowledge. Ps. 119:9-11 says: "How can a young man keep his way pure? By keeping it according to Thy Word. With all my heart I have sought Thee, do not let me wander from Thy commandments. Thy word I have treasured [hid] in my heart, that I may not sin against Thee." The faith that makes men free in Christ is certainly intelligent faith. Faith may go beyond reason, but not against it.

Even indirect knowledge involves proof of the truth of

judgments about reality, and proof entails logical certainty. Logical certainty is objective and universally valid, not just psychologically certain, although it is that. Certitude brings a psychical experience. The experience is not easily defined, but is most clearly seen in a willingness to act, which is discipleship. Paul Little says, "Our personal subjective experience is based on objective historical fact."[3] How can we know that we have not been taken in? That Christianity is true? Only if there is objective historical evidence for the claims of Christianity. Then, and only then, can we have a personal, internal experience – and *know* that it is valid.

Why is it that so many people "fall back on" an experiential religion? Because they have such a shallow knowledge of the real truth and evidence of Christianity. In such a case, the only thing they can do when challenged by circumstances or people is to retreat into their emotional experience. "I don't care what you say, this is how *I* feel." Emotional experience is not bad, or wrong, but for it to really be comforting in the Christian sense, it must be based on knowledge of the facts of the faith in Scripture and as history, We all start out our Christian walk as babes, to some extent or other, feeding on the milk, but none of us is expected to stay there. Paul even tells us to leave the elementary teachings of the faith and press on to maturity (Heb. 6:1). We are expected to be constantly growing in the knowledge of Christ.

Surely Jesus did not claim less than that His truth encompassed reality itself. Knowledge, then, both of Word and world, positive and negative, is prerequisite to freedom in Christ.

Mental Renewal Brings Transformation

In the New Testament, a higher and more spiritual service is to be rendered; not the sacrifice of animals, but the consecration of our whole beings. Rom. 12:1 says: "I urge you therefore, brethren, by the mercies of God, to present your bodies a living and holy sacrifice, acceptable to God, which is

---

[3]Paul E. Little, *Know Why You Believe* (Downers Grove, IL: InterVarsity, 1968), p. 103.

your spiritual service of worship." The believer is rationally to serve God in a lifelong process that involves the whole person. The Greek word here means worship, not an offering. Hodge writes: "It is not the thing offered that is said to be *reasonable* in the sense of endowed with reason, but the nature of the service. It is rendered by the mind."[4] Reasonable means "pertaining to the mind" and thus indicates a mental and spiritual service, not a ceremonial or external observance. Very plainly, acts of worship enfold our mental process.

Paul goes on to say: "And do not be conformed to this world, but be transformed by the renewing of your mind, that you may prove what the will of God is, that which is good and acceptable and perfect" (Rom. 12:2). We are to undergo a metamorphosis of mind for the purpose of *proving* and *approving* the will of God. The transformation to which we are exhorted is an entire alteration of the mental state. This alteration comes about as a constant testing, by the mind, of the data with which it is presented, and a continual reaffirming in its decisions of the will of God, "that which is good, acceptable, and perfect."

Christian growth must always involve knowledge and a resultant change of character. John R. W. Stott puts it this way:

> There are two main spheres in which the Christian is meant to grow. The first is in understanding and the second in holiness. When we begin the Christian life, we probably understand very little, and we have only just come to know God. Now we must increase in the knowledge of God and of our Lord and Savior, Jesus Christ. This knowledge is partly intellectual and partly personal. In connection with the former, I would urge you not only to study the Bible but to read good Christian books. To neglect to grow in your understanding is to court disaster.[5]

Knowledge is necessary not only for growth but to help us

---

[4]Charles Hodge, *Commentary on the Epistle to the Romans* (New York: A.C. Armstrong and Son, 1906), p. 604.

[5]John R. W. Stott, *Basic Christianity* (Downers Grove, IL: InterVarsity, 1968), pp. 136-137.

avoid intellectual and spiritual disaster.

Knowledge Issues in Love for God and Man

Paul's prayer for the Philippians was that their "love may abound still more and more in real knowledge and all discernment" (Phil. 1:9). It is through knowledge and discernment that a Christian's love becomes plentiful or wealthy in its fullness. The word here used for knowledge was almost a technical term that indicated knowledge *of* God, directed *to* God. The basis of this knowledge is the fact that God extended both revelation and salvation to man. Man's response to God is that of a vertical and horizontal love relationship.

God has given man grace, and man responds with faith and acceptance based on evidence. Now some theological systems tell us (supposedly from Eph. 2:8: "For by grace you have been saved through faith; and *that* not of yourselves, *it* is the gift of God") that "*faith* is a gift of God." The proponents of this view say the "that" and the "it" refer to the word *faith* and so clearly teach that faith is the gift of God. But in the Greek text of this passage there is only one pronoun, not two; and it does not agree grammatically with the word *faith*. The pronoun is neuter in gender, while faith is feminine. According to all grammatical rules, the gift cannot be faith. What is referred to here is God's gracious gift of salvation which none can merit. The Christian becomes the means of extending the love of God to other people as an ambassador of God in the ministry of reconciliation (2 Cor. 5:17-20; cf Matt. 28:18-20).

The word *discernment*, or insight, means intellectual understanding. In Paul's day this word had an established meaning, relating to the perception of good and evil in particular instances. Paul also says, in Heb. 5:14, that "solid food is for the mature, who *because of practice have their senses trained to discern good and evil*" [emphasis added]. Intellectual understanding is necessary for the Christian's ethical choices. God's will, in particular instances, is finally "a matter for the Christian himself to discern and decide, a matter of 'insight' into the given situation." For Paul this is not some vague moral instinct. Paul does not divorce insight from knowledge; they always go hand-in-hand. And both are nurtured by living in the community of believers.

> Believing in Christ means the acknowledgement that one belongs not to one's self but to Him, and belonging to Him means belonging to the body of Christ, the community of brethren who have been redeemed and claimed by the one Lord. This belonging to Christ and hence to one another is the presupposition and crucial preorientation of all believers' choosing and doing.[6]

What is done in any given circumstance must be based on our knowledge of God, on our love for God in Christ and love for our fellowman, and on our intellectual discernment into a particular event. Christians must learn the difference between hating the sin and loving the sinner both intellectually and practically. If Christ died for sinners just like us, and the Scriptures assure us that He did, then He loved the unlovely enough to give His life for them. We also are to love them. God will see to the judging when the time comes. Knowledge is essential for all love relationships.

The basis of man's need for knowledge is generally for his own salvation, for the day-to-day application of that knowledge in relationship with God in Christian living, for the growth of that relationship toward maturity (see 1 Cor. 3:1-2 and Heb. 5:13-14), and for the extension of God's love to other people that they also may know Him. Yes, knowledge is essential for us to truly be His disciples, and it frees us to really live for Him (1 Cor. 6:12-13; 10:23-24). Renewing the mind gives birth to change and maturity. Knowledge is essential for us to love both God and others.

---

[6]Victor Paul Furnish, *Theology and Ethics in Paul* (Nashville, TN: Abingdon, 1968), p. 237.

4 God's Image Shines In Us

Socrates is quoted as having said: "Let him that would move the world first move himself." We have always needed and will always need world movers. Therefore, I challenge some Christians to move themselves . . . and hopefully the world.
—*Reflections,* Vol. III

Thomas Aquinas once said that "reason in man is rather like God in the world." The nature of man, created in God's image; the nature of the Bible; the nature of deception, of doubting, and of maturity — all emphasize that man is related to God himself by the power of reason. The misuse of reason and/or knowledge caused man to be separated from his Creator. Aquinas went on to say: "We must say that man is possessed of free choice; otherwise, advice, exhortations, precepts, prohibitions, rewards, and punishments would be useless. . . . And so, man must be possessed of free choice, by the very fact that he is rational."[1]

Therefore, it is imperative that we reaffirm our need to know.

What It Means to Be Created in God's Image

It should be obvious from the beginning that God is *the rational being*. Man's creation in the image of God (Gen. 1:27) carries with it the particular ability of rationality or thought. Man, commonly defined as a rational animal, is responsible only because of his mind and what that entails: his capacity for knowing and discerning. The statement "God made man in His own image" logically implies that man's very nature is

---

[1]Vernon J. Bourke, *The Pocket Aquinas* (New York: Washington Square Press, 1960), p. 134.

such as to be rational.

A very important part of being created in God's image, and therefore being rational, is free will. For God to create us in His image, to delegate rationality to us of necessity entails that God has also delegated sovereignty to man, that is, the freedom to act and to be responsible for our actions. It is not uncommon for some philosophers to define freedom out of existence. Some use symbolic, or modal logic to prove man is determined and therefore not free. But such could hardly be the case. Just because the physicist has to stop motion to measure it doesn't mean there is no such thing as motion, anymore than just because the philosopher defines freedom out of existence, there is no such thing as freedom.

What is needed is a more rigorous empiricism. For it is obvious that we all experience reality as though we do indeed have free choice. The ability to know is itself evidence of freedom. As Samuel M. Thompson has said so well:

> That man is free we may be confident, as confident as we are that man is capable of knowing. For unless man is free, capable of some kind of genuine creative act, then he cannot know. He can only react, and his supposed awareness that he can react is only another reaction, and so on endlessly.... "Determinism is not, and never was, a working philosophy of life. One can conceivably die by it; not one ever consistently lived by it. If people would reflect more simply and sincerely on their actual experience of living they would be less vulnerable to a great deal of academic nonsense, and philosophy would be the gainer. In essence determinism is one of those theories which, as Professor Broad said of behaviorism, 'are so preposterously silly that only very learned men could have thought of them.' " Whether or not we are in fact free is a question only for those who wish to play games with concepts. Once we see what the question is we see that the very possibility of considering it *as a question to which true or false answers* may be given presupposes the fact of freedom.[2]

David Elton Trueblood quotes Lewis Mumford in this regard: "If man were 'just an animal' he would never have

---

[2]Samuel M. Thompson, *A Modern Philosophy of Religion* (Chicago, IL: Henry Regnery Co., 1955), pp. 178-179.

found that fact out."³

It has been said more than once that man is the only animal who laughs, the only one who weeps, the only one who prays, the only one who walks fully erect, the only one who makes fires, the only one who can invent, the only one with a written language, the only one who is proud, the only one who can make progress, the only one who guides his own destiny, the only one who is penitent, and the only one who needs to be.⁴ Man is unique by virtue of the very fact that he puzzles about his uniqueness. Man is part of nature, but he is also more than nature. Yes, we have appetites, but we can deny their satisfaction by conscious purpose to the extent that a human being can actually willfully starve to death.

Freedom, then, is crucial.⁵ The gift of freedom enters into almost every distinct human experience. "It bears, for example, upon the reality of sin, because the fact that man *can* sin represents a remarkable ability. No other creature known to us can sin at all. . . . The heart of positive freedom is the twin experience of *deliberation* and *decision*."⁶ As one systematic theologian has said, "To say that the stronger motive always prevails is an empty tautology, since the test by which a motive is proved stronger is simply that it prevails."⁷

"Knowledge is a guide, but not, in its role as knowledge, a cause." The example has been given of a music score. It may guide the musician's performance, but it does not cause his performance.

> He may follow it or not, as his ability permits and as he pleases. It makes no difference to the score whether he plays the music or not, and it makes no difference to the musical

---

³David Elton Trueblood, *Philosophy of Religion* (New York: Harper & Row, 1957), p. 275.
⁴*Ibid.*
⁵A much fuller treatment of the issue of free will versus determinism needs to be done than can be handled here. I suggest reading, as a beginning, chapter 11 the section entitled "Man's Freedom" and chapter 28 the section entitled "Human Freedom and God" in Thompson's *A Modern Philosophy of Religion* and chapter 19 in Trueblood's *Philosophy of Religion*.
⁶Trueblood, *ibid.*, pp. 277-278.
⁷See Paul Tillich's *Systematic Theology*, vol. 1, p. 184.

meaning of the score. The score is not itself a part of the performance. It is only a guide which the player may follow. If a music score caused the player to follow it then to learn to play a musical instrument would be an easy matter.[8]

Insofar as man is free, he can act in a way which is considered appropriate to the occasion or in a way which is not, but obviously he can choose. Thompson goes on to say:

> The confusion concerning causes and occasions is a part of the same misunderstanding which enables some philosophers to consider cognition as itself only one among man's many reactions to stimuli. Knowledge, on this view, is just another effect of causes operating on the organism, and it in turn is the cause of other effects. Knowledge, in short, is considered simply one of the connecting links in the causal chain of human behavior. This is only one more way in which philosophical naturalism commits its characteristic fallacy, the fallacy of mistaking essence for existence.[9]

There are many obvious difficulties with determinism. It is faced with two "tremendous contradictions." (1) The contradiction concerning truth. If we are to take determinism seriously, it would necessitate the idea that all intellectual judgment is itself determined. This would have to apply even to the judgment that determinism is true. "The damning fact about mechanistic determinism is that it undermines the possibility of truth and yet claims to be true."

> The climax of this criticism is that determinism provides no intelligible theory of error. It holds that error occurs and is, indeed, extremely common, inasmuch as so many people have not become convinced determinists, but it does not tell us how error is possible, how error can be detected, or even what error is.

(2) Causal determinism destroys "the very planning on which so much store is set." The determinist does not like the fact that freedom to decide "brings in an incalculable element that the planner seeks to avoid." Yet if complete determinism is

---

[8]Thompson, *A Modern Philosophy of Religion*, p. 184.
[9]*Ibid.*, p. 185.

true, the very idea of planning is itself undermined.

> The paradox which the planner must face, however, if he is intellectually alert, *is that in the terms of his philosophy his very effort to plan was itself also determined by prior conditions.* Therefore, he does not actually plan at all, but is merely the helpless and passive performer of deeds which are materially necessitated. It is generally supposed that, by taking careful thought, we can make a better world, but men and women who are truly convinced of the determinist creed cannot be influenced by such foolishness.[10]

Human freedom is no restriction upon God's power. Exactly the opposite is in fact true: "If God had to negate man's freedom and force him to choose in the proper way, then His omnipotence truly would be compromised." Freedom, again, in man is delegated sovereignty freely given by God to man because we are created in His image.

> Perhaps the basic error in the notion that there is an inconsistency in asserting both human freedom and divine omnipotence is the idea that God's power is a kind of compulsion, exerted upon and against other things. It should be plain to us, even from our own limited experience, that external coercion is the very feeblest of all forces when used against another's wIL You may force another to act in a certain way, but you cannot by force bring him to desire to do what you have determined he shall do, or to mean what you compel him to say. The stronger his will the further does your compulsion alienate him from your purposes. You may break his will, but then his acquiescence is not truly his act. If God is truly omnipotent He does not force man's will; rather He enlists it. Even when man's will remains defiant, God turns that defiance to His own purpose.[11]

As one philosopher of history has put it, "Man's freedom, his capacity for genuine decision, is taken as fundamental, for without it there could be neither religion nor ethics."[12] And

---

[12]Trueblood, *Philosophy of Religion*, pp. 279-282.
[11]Thompson, *A Modern Philosophy of Religion*, p. 503.
[12]See Will Herberg's *Judaism and Modern Man*, p. 92 also quoted in Trueblood, *Philosophy of Religion*, p. 289.

as Trueblood has said, "Without the recognition of freedom we should have a woefully inadequate conception, not only of man, but likewise of God."[13]

Freedom is only meaningful in the light of the being and nature of God. We are free only because our freedom is derived from being created in the image of God. God is certainly free in ways that we are not, "The crucial difference is revealed in the observation that man makes nothing that is free.... The omnipotence of God is shown in the fact that He alone has made free beings."[14] Yet, though our freedom is different, limited as compared to God's, to *be* (in the sense of created in God's image) is to be free and to be free is to be able to create, both for God and for man.

God is a personal being. Much of the biblical language about God uses personal categories. R. T. France describes what it means to be personal:

> A person is a conscious being, one who thinks, feels, and purposes, and carries these purposes into action, one who has active relationships with others — you can talk to a person, and get a response; you can share feelings and ideas with him, argue with him, love him, hate him; you can *know* him, in a way which can only be described as "personal!"[15]

Creation in God's image carries with it all the responsibilities of personhood described above.

God is a living being. He is actively present here and now. This is seen in the very name of God (Ex. 3:14, 15). The Hebrew word "to be" signifies a dynamic, active presence. God is actively related to man; and man, by being created in God's image, is actively related to God. Thus being created in God's image enables man to embrace *His* rationality and *His* freedom and *His* personality, and to have a capacity for a spiritual relationship with God.

---

[13]Trueblood, *Philosophy of Religion*, p. 289.
[14]*Ibid.*, p. 290.
[15]R.T. France, *The Living God* (Downers Grove, IL: InterVarsity Press, 1970), pp. 19,20.

The Nature of Propositional Revelation

The Bible claims, more than three thousand times, its own inspiration.[16] "The category *revelation* ... refers to the divine self-disclosure, the purpose of which is, by intervention in history and communication in language, the calling of men into fellowship with God."[17] *Propositional revelation* is the claim that the truth of God is recorded for man in sentence form, in human language. When Christian theologians say that the Bible is propositional revelation, the claim is that God has communicated truth about reality as such in the sentence structure of human language and that this truth is eternally valid.

If the Bible is really God's divine self-disclosure, then the content of its sentences give us information that is absolutely, eternally true. The very nature of Scripture as the special revelation of God necessitates man's use of his mental capacities. Because the Bible was written in human language, we must use the capabilities of our minds to read and understand what it says. Thus there is no substitute for detailed study of the Scriptures using the same methods one would use to study any other written document.

God has given Scripture to mankind in the medium of a particular language, at a particular point in time, in the words of men using idioms and imagery. What sense could it possibly make for God to give men minds, communicate His will to them in human language, and then not expect them to study what has been revealed? Dinsdale T. Young, a British Methodist, said it this way:

> One of the great presuppositions of the Bible is that God's people will read. The existence of Scripture is in itself an argument for the necessity of reading. That God inspired a book indicated His desire that His servants should be readers.[18]

---

[16]John H. Gerstner, *Reasons for Faith* (Grand Rapids, MI: Baker Book House, 1967), pp. 69-70.

[17]Clark H. Pinnock, *Biblical Revelation: The Foundation of Christian Theology* (Chicago, IL: Moody Press, 1971), p. 29.

[18]Dinsdale T. Young, *Messages for Home and Life* (London, 1907), p. 61 quoted in Wilbur M. Smith's *Chats From a Minister's Library* (Grand Rapids, MI: Baker Book House, 1951), p. 175.

Assuredly man has a need to know, based on the very existence of propositional revelation.

Deception Is a Mental Act

When Satan deceives a man, he does it mentally (cf. 2 Cor. 2:11; 3:14; 4:4; 10:5). It is our *minds*, our thoughts, that are "led astray from the simplicity and purity of devotion to Christ" (2 Cor. 11:3). Certainly knowledge can be misused. Right knowledge, that is, correct understanding, should prevent the Christian from wandering from the path of truth. The cognitive elements of Christianity can prevent the choosing of the road of subtle deception. The best defense is always a good offense. Knowing *why* we believe *what* we believe is essential to the Christian life in all respects. One who knows the way has a surer journey than the man who has not unrolled the map.

In fact, one of the ideas that Christians are most deceived about is what constitutes proof, or what can be "proven." I even know some Christian philosophers, friends, who have a misunderstanding about this. Perhaps you have heard some person say, about matters of the Christian faith, "You can't *prove* that; it's only something you believe!" Of course, what they are really saying is this: Only things that can be known with absolute certainty can be proved. In other words, according to the modern mind, unless there is scientific evidence, empirical data, something cannot be known as a fact.

Of course this view has a *very* limited conception of what constitutes proof. It turns out that most of what people accept as reality — historical fact, relationships, most everyday experiences — cannot be proven on this basis. It also turns out that even scientific evidence is understood in terms of a world view. There are presuppositions, philosophical assumptions, behind how we "do" science. Thus broad ranges of what we claim as scientific knowledge cannot be known with absolute certainty.

My son, even as a high-school freshman, saw through this double standard in regard to what constitutes "proof." He was given an assignment in his Survey of World Literature class to write on the following topic.

Can It Be Proven Beyond a Shadow of a Doubt That a Heavenly Paradise Is a Matter of Fact?

There are many writers in history that deal with the question of whether there is a heaven — philosophers, poets, priests, etc. This is a very "tricky" question to answer. First we need to decide what is meant by "prove," "beyond a shadow of a doubt" and "matter of fact." If we define these terms the way we normally do in everyday usage, one would want to answer no! Yet, this answer already assumes certain views about knowledge and the world in which we live.

If by "prove" we mean to use the word as modern science uses it, then again the answer would be no. The scientist believes that something cannot be "proven," "beyond a shadow of a doubt," "as a matter of fact" to exist unless it can be reproduced in a laboratory by correct method. Certainly no one can reproduce heaven in a laboratory by the scientific method. Scientists prove that something exists by observing it using the five senses. Again, obviously no one can feel, see, hear, taste, or smell heaven. Therefore, there is no "scientific way" of proving heaven "beyond a shadow of a doubt," "as a matter of fact." Of course, there is some question as to how "certainly" something can be proven even in the modern scientific way. Modern science rests on assumptions about the physical world that cannot be proven by the laboratory method either.

If what we mean by "prove" is not limited to the modern scientific method, then the answer can be yes. The ways humans claim to have access to truth or "knowledge" is not now, nor has it ever been, limited to only the scientific method, or the "empirical method." We claim to know for sure many things, about many different fields of study, that we cannot "prove" by modern science; for example: historical facts, psychology, emotions, the basis of mathematics, etc. One of the divisions of philosophy is called "epistemology" — "how we know what we know." Scholars have always claimed to have certain knowledge apart from the modern scientific method.

Thus to decide a question about the actual existence of heaven, one must look at the evidence in terms of a world view. A "world view" is a perspective of life, conception of things or "a comprehensive conception or apprehension of the world, especially from a specific standpoint." If there is excellent evidence to support the claims of a Christian world view in history and in terms of how one judges "truth claims" in relation to world view claims, then it would be possible to know "beyond a shadow of a doubt," "as a matter of fact" that there is a heaven. C. S. Lewis once said that "faith" [in the

Christian sense — evidence for what is believed] can reach a level where there is a psychological exclusion of doubt, but one never stops being willing to re-examine the evidence.

What we view as proof has always been different, depending on whether we were talking about proof in science, history, law, journalism or theology. In history, for instance, proof is (1) all known evidence is in favor of that particular historical claim; (2) the absence of viable alternative theories; and (3) (though not needed, it is helpful) this particular historical claim has stood the test of time.

In fact, the scientific method based on inductive logic, or the inductive method, *cannot* yield "absolute certainty" — perhaps high probability, but only probability nonetheless. Any logician will confirm what I have just said. The point is that you cannot get absolute certainty from the scientific method; therefore it is not valid to require by way of proof in history or matters of the faith absolute certainty either. Christians, of course, claim that we *do* have empirical evidence for the claims of Christianity by way of the historical evidence for the resurrection of Jesus that can be judged like any history.

Knowledge Controls Doubt

Knowledge, both biblical and secular, is needed to regulate and restrain doubting and to prevent the Christian from stagnating because of unresolved questionings. Peter's doubts put him in physical peril (Matt. 14:22-32). The double-minded man puts himself in spiritual peril (James 1:7, 8). Jesus' injunction against worry is rooted in the fact that those who are overly concerned with this world's benefits are allowing their thoughts to be controlled by these benefits (Matt. 6:25-30).

Many people misunderstand Matt. 6:25-30 to say that a Christian should not be concerned about using his mind. They make the mistake of equating thinking with worry. "After all," they say, "the trouble with the 'men of little faith' was that they questioned God. One should not think about the 'why' of spiritual things, but only accept them." I quoted D. Martyn Lloyd-Jones' penetrating insight in regard to this passage's real teaching earlier in this book, but perhaps a longer quote would be helpful here:

> Faith, according to our Lord's teaching in this paragraph, is primarily thinking; and the whole trouble with a man of little faith is that he does not think. He allows circumstances to bludgeon him.... We must spend more time in studying our Lord's lessons in observation and deduction. The Bible is full of logic, and we must never think of faith as something purely mystical. We do not just sit down in an armchair and expect marvelous things to happen to us. That is not Christian faith. Christian faith is essentially thinking... Faith, if you like, can be defined like this: It is a man insisting upon thinking when everything seems determined to... knock him down in an intellectual sense. The trouble with the person of little faith is that, instead of controlling his own thought, his thought is being controlled by something else.... That is the essence of worry.... That is not thought; that is the absence of thought, a failure to think.[19]

What seems on the surface to be against using the mind is an exhortation, by Christ, to think. It is imperative for the Christian to develop intellectual content in order to know why this idea or position is acceptable and that one not. The seeker of truth who uses his doubts as a motivation to find honest answers must not be disheartened, Rather, the doubter who stagnates in his pool of unresolved questions has found his excuse in his complacency with ignorance. The very real effects of doubting or worry underline the Christian's need to know.

Knowledge Fosters Maturity

The Christian's need to know is revealed as explicit in the process of maturing in Christ. Paul considered his teaching "milk" — aimed at calling Christians to surrender themselves to God; missionary preaching — as opposed to "solid food," that is, teaching the full richness and magnificence of the gospel to convinced Christians (1 Cor. 3:2). And again "solid

---

[19]D. Martyn Lloyd-Jones, *Studies in the Sermon on the Mount*, vol. 2 (Grand Rapids, MI: Eerdmans, 1960), pp. 126-130.

food is for the mature, who because of practice have their senses trained to *discern* good and evil" (Heb. 5:11-14; see also 1 Pet. 2:2, and John 16:12). Discernment means intellectual content.

The Christian's need to know is revealed as implicit in the process established for equipping saints and building the body of Christ (Eph. 4:11-12). The testimony of the apostles; the fore- and forth-telling prophets; the proclamation of the good news of Christ by the evangelist; and the shepherding, teaching function of the pastor-teacher all carry an essential cognitive element that contributes to the maturation of the individual and of the corporate body, the Church of Jesus Christ.

Man's need to know is a result of his rational and spiritual creation in God's image; of the Bible as propositional revelation; of deception as a mental process that must be combated mentally; and of the role of knowledge explicitly and implicitly in the process of maturing.

5 Building the Faith in Our World

The Church has three grand tasks which are never complete, and which embody its very reason for existing: worship, praising God in all aspects of life; discipling, teaching its own to mature in Christ; and evangelism, teaching others the good news of God's love.
—*Reflections*, Vol. I

The degree to which a Christian has a need to know is readily seen in the benefits of knowledge for the individual Christian and to the kingdom of Christ. "It would even be safe to say not only that some people *should* be Christian philosophers, they *must*. For a philosophically inclined person who is also a Christian, doing philosophy of religion is a spiritual necessity."[1] Every believer has a responsibility to be able to *support* and *defend* what he or she believes. This does not mean that every believer must be a scholar or an expert, but it does mean that every Christian has a responsibility to be growing constantly during his lifetime so that he knows more about his belief. To do this, every Christian should always be involved in Bible study and have access to good literature that can help provide answers to important questions.

Knowledge performs *three important functions* that enable the believer not only to grow in Christian maturity but also to relate his faith to the people around him. Knowledge *confirms* faith in believers; an individual's faith is firmly established, verified, only when Christianity becomes an increasingly evident way of life for the believer. Knowledge *communicates* faith to unbelievers; knowing why you are a Christian and

---

[1] See Stephen T. Davis's paper entitled "Philosophy, Christianity, and Religious Faith," published by InterVarsity Christian Fellowship, 233 Langdon St., Madison, WI 53703.

what it is to be one is necessary if one is to impart it to others. And knowledge *defends* faith to unbelievers; it is not enough in most cases simply to communicate the facts of Christianity to unbelievers, we must be able to support our faith with reasons for it.

Knowledge Confirms Faith in Believers

Knowledge is necessary to prove the truth or validity of the Christian faith in at least three ways. Initially, knowledge is necessary as a *ground* or basis for faith. By that I mean a solid foundation upon which one can build. No matter how one comes to an acceptance of Jesus as Lord and Savior (as a very young child or from a "foxhole" or emotional experience), there is a *constant need* to strengthen the foundation upon which the acceptance is built.

Ideally this foundation should be in construction even before conversion, but certainly it must — for the sake of the new believer — be in formation as early as possible. Even when taken to be simple belief in something, faith assumes a certain knowledgeable content. Richard Purtill writes that faith must be based on good reasons. Belief, in the sense of Christian faith, has the following characteristics: "We must have some understanding of what we claim to believe; we must be prepared to take action appropriate to our stated belief; and we must have some reason for belief."[2]

Second, knowledge should *extend* our faith. Faith, whatever we mean by the word, should increase as our knowledge of the thing believed increases and as our confidence in its objective truth increases. If Christianity is true, as surely all Christians think it is, then we should be willing to test it against all other claims in all marketplaces. Certainly we have the Apostle Paul's example in this (see Acts, ch. 17). It is only in this way that our faith can reach the level, again according to C. S. Lewis,[3] where we do not have psychological doubt,

---

[2] Richard Purtill, *Reasons to Believe* (Grand Rapids, MI: Eerdmans, 1974), p. 72.

[3] C. S. Lewis, on "Obstinacy in Belief" in *The World's Last Night and Other Essays* (New York: Harcourt Brace Jovanovich, Inc., 1965), p. 16.

but are constantly willing to reexamine the evidence in any marketplace.

Third, it is also by this constant examination of our faith in light of other claims that knowledge *affirms* our faith. Faith is in this way shown not to be credulity, or gullibility. Christians can thus accept the truth of Christianity not only because of the evidence for its specific doctrinal claims, but because it makes sense out of everything else he knows.[4] If Christianity is objectively valid, it must really make sense of things. It must give the believer a viable world view (*weltanschauung*) by which to assess the fitness of things. Seeing the Christian faith as a world view is perhaps the highest level of faith and certainly demands the most confirmation in regard to the Christian's need to know.[5]

Knowledge Communicates Faith to Unbelievers

Intelligent use of knowledge is prerequisite to proper witnessing. The Christian lives a dual life: one in spiritual communion with God and other Christians in fellowship, and the other in daily contact with the unbelieving world. The unbeliever forms judgments of the believer from what he observes the Christian say and do in his everyday life. Therefore we have a twofold admonition.

Regarding content: We have the solemn responsibility to conduct ourselves with *wisdom* toward unbelievers to make the most of every witness opportunity. We are told, in Col. 4:5, "Conduct yourselves with *wisdom* toward outsiders, *making the most of the opportunity*" (emphasis added). Wisdom, again, is good judgment based on knowledge. It is knowledge applied to individual situations in which other human beings are involved. Knowing *what* to say, *how* to say it, and *when* to say it is very important in effective witnessing. Obviously there must be a clear, intelligent understanding of what we

---

[4]Purtill, *Reasons to Believe*, p. 76.
[5]See James W Sire, *The Universe Next Door: A Basic World View Catalog* (Downers Grove, IL: InterVarsity Press, 1976) and Norman L. Geisler and William Watkin's *Perspectives: Understanding and Evaluating Today's World Views* (San Bernardino, CA : Here's Life Publishers, Inc., 1984).

believe in order to communicate it effectively. If we are going to engage in meaningful dialogue, we need to know the unbelievers' position as well, or perhaps better, than they. The content responsibility of a Christian relates not only to "internal" content — how we live because of what we are inside — but also to "external" content — how we respond because of what we know.

Regarding style: The Christian's life should be instructive to the unbeliever in both word and deed. We have a responsibility to *know* how to respond to each person with gracious speech. Col. 4:6 says: "Let your speech always be with grace, seasoned, as it were, with salt, so that you may *know* how you should respond to each person" (emphasis added; cf. 1 Pet. 3:15). The unbeliever must see God's grace through us. The basic idea of *charis* (grace) here is beauty, charm, or graciousness. We should apply our intellectual content wisely at all times with kindness, courtesy and compassion. The two sides of Christian witness — content and style — paint for the unbeliever a beautiful picture of our Lord's life while on earth and make for effective witness that, hopefully, results in effective evangelism. (I will say more on this in the next chapter.)

Knowledge Defends Faith to Unbelievers

This is the realm of Christian apologetics. We have a quantity and a quality of "evidence that demands a verdict,"[6] The Greek word *apologia* means an intellectual defense of the truth of one's position. It is used eight times in the New Testament: 1 Pet. 3:15, where we are told to "always be ready to make a defense to every one who asks you to give an account for the hope that is in you, yet with gentleness and reverence"; in Acts 22:1 Paul tells his listeners to "hear my defense which I now offer to you"; in Acts 25:16 Paul says that it was not the Roman custom "to hand over any man before . . . [he] has an opportunity to make his defense against the charges"; 1 Cor 9:3, where Paul makes his defense of his apostleship; 2 Cor 7:11, where Paul writes ". . . what vin-

---

[6]The title of Josh McDowell's book, published by Campus Crusade for Christ, 1972.

dication of yourselves [defense] . . . in everything you demonstrated yourselves to be innocent in the matter"; in 2 Tim. 4:16, where Paul states that at his "defense no one supported" him; and Phil. 1:7, 17, where Paul writes that he defended and was "appointed for the defense of the gospel."

Christian apologetics has a twofold task in any age. First, responsibility to destroy "speculations and every lofty thing raised up against the knowledge of God," and to take "every thought captive to the obedience of Christ" (2 Cor. 10:5). Christians have a scriptural obligation to demolish sophistries and plausible fallacies with which men evade the teachings of Christianity. These evadings are rationalizations that are not logically valid, or at least not logically necessary. They, therefore, can be shown to be in error.[7]

It must be stressed that this is not a warfare *with* weapons or *against* persons. Christians have no right to use their knowledge to show themselves off or to put down the unbeliever. As Christians we are not playing mental games. If as Christians, we cannot afford the luxury of ignorance, neither can we afford the luxury of arrogance. We should exercise the use of our knowledge because the love of God for lost souls is at issue, not just to win arguments. These are arguments and ideas that must be shown to be in error, or "destroyed," in order to win over those who hold them. Christians have no warrant to destroy the reasoners to stop the reasoning. When an atheistic philosophy is pressing for control, the Christian, as Thomas Aquinas indicated, needs to philosophize harder in order to show the error of the false philosophy. Again we see that the Christian's need for knowledge is broader than just knowledge of his own beliefs, time and culture.

And regarding the second task of Christian apologetics, it is our responsibility to be always "ready to make a defense to every one who asks" (1 Pet. 3:15). The use of the word "always" indicates that *cramming* is not sufficient here. Christian education must be about teaching us systematically

---

[7]See Wilbur M. Smith's *Therefore Stand: A Plea for a Vigorous Apologetic in This Critical Hour of the Christian Faith* (Natick, MA: W.A. Wilde Co., 1945).

to synthesize material so that we shall be able by cognitive processes to deduce conclusions based on how our knowledge fits individual situations. Proof texts and "pat" answers are never sufficient. Once we have shown the error in another position, we must go on to support our own. It is not enough to say, "This is why yours is wrong." We must, in doing that, also be able to give reasons why ours is right — and to any man who asks. Christian apologetics as seen in the New Testament certainly emphasizes the believer's need to know.

6 Free to Win Souls to Christ

I do not think one can truly be "In Christ" unless that person has a burning desire to change the world toward the Christian ideal!
—*Reflections,* Vol. I

Recently, two of my colleagues and I were having lunch with William Bentley Ball, one of the foremost constitutional lawyers in our country. William Ball has argued nineteen cases before the United States Supreme Court as well as in twenty-two states and is a great defender of religious freedom in America. I asked Mr. Ball what was the most important thing that could be done to help our society today. Without hesitation, Mr. Ball replied: that individuals come to know Jesus as their Lord and Savior. We can only have a "burning desire to change the world toward the Christian ideal" if we are serious about evangelism. Only when people are changed will our world be changed.

Yet so many today see evangelism as an emotional, rather than an intelligent, process. It is certainly more than "intelligence" (the Holy Spirit is essential), but definitely not less. Several aspects of Christian experience relate to the Christian's need to know regarding evangelism or "soul winning." *Evangelism,* which is certainly of prime importance, has to be based on knowledge both of God and of the world. We live in a world that has so embraced cultural and intellectual relativism that we have forgotten the function of reason in conversion.[1]

Some folks even deny that argument, correctly or falsely

---

[1] See Francis Schaeffer, *Escape From Reason* (Downers Grove, IL: InterVarsity Press, 1968) for a good elementary treatment, though it has problems regarding specific disciplines.

used, can lead to or away from belief. Unfortunately, we twentieth-century Christians have been widely exposed to the idea that reason is not important to our faith or to implanting faith in others. We need once again to realize how essential knowledge is to giving Christ His proper place in our world. There are many Christians, even some of my students, who feel all that is important is the "practical." They do not realize that the practice always rests on some foundation — or "theory." If the theory is false or misunderstood it will undermine the effectiveness, or truth, of their practice.

Evangelism Is Intelligent

Intelligent evangelism does not require each Christian to be a complete storehouse of knowledge. The educated man is one who is able to relate one discipline to another, not just display technical knowledge in one field. Intelligence has been defined as "the ability to adapt readily to new and different situations." Such ability arises clearly, and more readily, out of a broad background of knowledge and experience. Paul displayed such an ability, growing out of his Jewish education, which, as Richard Longnecker aptly phrased it, "sought to produce a man who could think and act, one who was neither an egghead nor a clod."[2]

Paul, from whom we derive the New Testament pattern for missionary action, "according to his custom . . . reasoned . . . from the Scripture" (Acts 18:1-4, 17-34). The word here translated "reasoned" means to discourse, to calculate, to argue on, to practice dialectic; elicit conclusions by discussion. The word was often used of logicians. He also quoted the Athenians' own historians and poets (v. 28) in making his defense of Christianity. Paul's practice was to reason or "argue" the scriptural and factual basis for his faith. Should we do less?

We see clearly the response to Paul's actions (Acts 17:32-34), but before I say something about that response, perhaps, it would be good if we looked closer at the narrative. We have

---

[2]Richard Longnecker, *The Ministry and Message of Paul* (Grand Rapids, MI: Zondervan Publishing House, 1971), p. 22.

already learned that it was Paul's custom to reason with people about the truth of Christianity. Surely this tells us something about the need for intelligent evangelism. Paul started this reasoning process in the synagogue (Acts 17:1-2) with the Jews and God-fearing Gentiles, and branched out to "the marketplace every day with those who happened to be present" (v. 17). Paul started where there was a likelihood that his audience might be most receptive, that is, where they shared the same high monotheism, and then he worked out from there. We also learn in this passage that instead of condemning his listeners, though he was angered because they knew better, Paul appealed to the truth that they had (vv. 22-23) and the common ground that they shared (vv. 27-29).

Then Paul went to Athens, waiting for Silas and Timothy (vv. 15-16). Wilbur Smith says of this visit: "Into the university city of the world some time in August, A.D. 51, there came a man on foot, about fifty years of age, a Jew, who had probably never been heard of in this center of intellectual preeminence, by the name of Paul."[3] On one of the days that he was reasoning with people in the marketplace he met "some of the Epicurean and Stoic philosophers" who were present (v. 18). It is clear, from their reaction, that these philosophers were not calling Paul a "babbler" as we would use the term, for "they took him and brought him to the Areopagus, saying, 'May we know what this new teaching is which you are proclaiming?' " (vv. 19-20) because he was teaching about Jesus and His resurrection. In taking Paul to the Areopagus, the Epicurean and Stoic philosophers were according Paul a very high honor. This was the place where all the important scholars in residence and visiting scholars were invited to lecture on the newest knowledge (v. 21).

In Acts 17:22-31, we have only a small part of Paul's address to the scholars of Athens. Paul told them about the nature of the one God they themselves acknowledged and that this God, whom they worshiped as unknown, had made Himself known through Jesus. Paul went on to tell them that

---

[3] Wilbur M. Smith, *Therefore Stand: A Plea for a Vigorous Apologetic in This Critical Hour of the Christian Faith* (Natick, ME: W.A. Wilde Co., 1945), p. 246.

God had verified the message and the messenger — Jesus — by raising Him from the dead (vv. 31-32) and that they should repent (v. 30). But what about the philosophers' reaction to Paul? Was Paul a failure in Athens? I have heard minister after minister say that Paul was such a miserable failure in Athens that when he went to the Corinthians, he vowed never to use this method — reason and philosophy — again, but only "to preach the gospel, not in cleverness of speech" (1 Cor. 1:17). If I cannot do anything else in this book, I pray that I can put that nonsense to rest once and for all.

Wilbur Smith, in his book *Therefore Stand*, writes:

> I believe that the Apostle Paul was as definitely led of the Holy Spirit to utter this particular discourse on Mars' Hill as he was to give his apologies before Festus or Agrippa, or to preach any of the sermons that ever proceeded from his lips throughout his thirty years of powerful presentation of the Gospel. *We must recognize in the first place that the results of this address were not, even then, altogether nil; some were saved that day, which would be a dual miracle, considering the audience he had to speak to.* [Emphasis added.] There were a few even of the notable people of the city who believed, as a result of Paul's address. Would to God that on every occasion that you and I had even spoken it could be said that some believed, noble or ignoble! . . . It should be remembered that even our Lord did not always have results.

Smith goes on to say:

> The question now must be faced: why were the results of Paul's powerful, magnificent address on Mars' Hill so meager? . . . [We need to be] reminded that . . . while the ancient Greeks had an extremely rare appreciation for the beauties of nature, for the marvels, for statuary, and paintings, for the development of the human body, for conversation, and speculation, they had lost any mood of seriousness in their pursuit of life. . . . As it was in Athens in the days of Paul, so it is now in our own university centers. In the great city of Cambridge, Massachusetts, in the halls of Harvard University, let anyone who loves the Gospel stand up and tell how pitifully feeble would be the immediate consequences of the proclamation of a crucified and risen Saviour within hearing of that student body. What hearing does the *Gospel* have in New Haven? . . . I do not mean that there are not some true believers within the

environments of these cities — there were some in Athens, but oh! how few and for the most part how hard to reach those living in these citadels of intellectualism.[4]

Was Paul a failure in Athens? Of course not, how ridiculous to say so. To say that Paul, a man under the guidance of the Holy Spirit, made a mistake under divine inspiration in this most important case of presenting the gospel and had to repent has devastating consequences to any theory of inspiration and revelation. Though I am sure that those who preach that Paul was mistaken here have never thought of this.

There is nothing in the Corinthian correspondence to indicate that what Paul meant by "not in cleverness of speech" was that preaching or witnessing should not use reason or evidence or relate the gospel to the things of the world. Remember, too, that the context of the Corinthian correspondence was a message to a church that needed some serious help with its doctrine, not with conversion-a church that was misusing knowledge to justify living according to the flesh and not according to the knowledge of the teachings of the apostle and the Holy Spirit.

This idea, that Paul was a failure, is just simply wrong. Yes, "some began to sneer." But the text plainly tells us Paul had converts from that august audience. And if I understand the New Testament, then every time the gospel is preached — regardless of whether there are immediate results — a victory occurs for God. If Paul was a failure, we should all be such failures!

Argument Can Lead to Conversion

Scripture shows repeatedly that mere proclamation of the gospel alone did not account for its acceptance. Apostolic witness in Scripture declares again and again the evidential and historical nature of Christianity. Reasoning and argument were used to bring about conversions (Acts 18:4; 9:26-31). As Clark Pinnock so clearly shows:

---

[4]*Ibid.*, ch. 6, "St. Paul's Address to the Athenian Philosophers," especially pp. 259-261.

> People are constantly affected in their actions and choices by arguments, intelligent or otherwise. The notion that nobody is ever converted to Christ by argument is a foolish platitude. It would be more accurate to say that the reason so few people are being converted to Him now is that so many Christians believe the fallacy. It is high time for us to restock the arsenal of Christian evidences and confront our contemporaries with a solid message.[5]

No person who has taught or has sat in a university classroom can believe that fallacy; nor can such a one fail to realize the importance that argument can play in an individual's beliefs. (By "argument" I do not mean "being argumentative" or "argument for argument's sake," but *reasoning*.) Arguing the rational validity of one's position is not the same as being argumentative.

Can we expect men to accept the poignant moral implications of the Christian message merely on the basis of our personal testimony? Certainly such important claims must be based on more than personal feelings. They must be supported by the knowledgeable evidence of reason! This support the apostles provided throughout New Testament times, and this we should provide throughout our lives.

Knowledge Can Build the Faith in the World

We need to give God's Word its proper place in the world. This can be done through sound Christian scholarship. We must secure the best quality young men and women of every generation to fill the halls of our great academic institutions, to lift the banners of Christian scholarship high to their Lord before the eyes of the world. Only when each Christian scholar accepts the responsibility for duplicating himself in at least one or two of his brightest students each year will he be taking his scholarship and his Lord seriously.

> The hour has struck for a renaissance in Christian letters, and the training of a body of articulate apologists. We need a group of well-trained scholars capable of following the myths

---

[5] Clark H. Pinnock, *Set Forth Your Case: An Examination of Christianity's Credentials* (Chicago, IL: Moody Press, 1967), p. 126.

of our day to their source, and exposing them there. Their ministry would include traveling from city to city, and university to university, defending the whole faith and presenting the evidence for its validity. Out of their midst would come a library of new literature in every area of theological concern, which would spark a revival in life and truth throughout the length and breadth of the Christian church.[6]

This will happen only when Christians everywhere, on all levels, become serious about Christian education. The change must come about, and we believe it is coming about. The battle will not be easy; indeed it never has been easy. The task requires more effort than many are willing to give. Thousands must shake off their cultural, educational and institutional apathy and form a mighty army of Christian scholars to infiltrate all levels of the church and the world for and in the name of Jesus, the Christ.

But Let's Be Practical

"This all sounds nice," you say, "but it is so idealistic and impractical." Perhaps so, but the very existence of Christianity today indicated what God has always been able to do with a few dedicated people through the Holy Spirit. If I am idealistic I am in good company. The apostles and many others in more recent church history have been just as idealistic about the Christian's need to know. Two examples, one biblical and one from more recent history, will suffice to prove the point.

Many scholars think 2 Tim. 4:13 was one of the last passages of Scripture Paul ever wrote, dictated while in prison at Rome, and near the time of his death. It shows Paul's love for books and their contents.[7] Paul asked Timothy to bring him the "books" and "parchments." The parchments were probably rolls of Old Testament Scripture or perhaps copies of Christ's words, or Luke, or Acts. The books are generally thought to have been Greek and Latin manuscripts of favorite authors, poets, historians. Charles H. Spurgeon says this of the request:

---

[6]*Ibid.*, p. 127.
[7]Wilbur M. Smith, *Chats From the Ministers Library,* ch. 13, "Paul's Love of Books" (Grand Rapids, MI: Baker Book House, 1951), pp. 169-186.

> He [the Apostle Paul] is inspired and yet he wants books! . . . He has seen the Lord, and yet he wants books! He has had a wider experience than most men, and yet he wants books! . . . The Apostle says to Timothy and so he says to every preacher, "Give thyself unto reading." The man who never reads will never be read; he who never quotes will never be quoted. He who will not use the thoughts of other men's brains, proves that he has no brains of his own. Brethren, what is true of ministers is true of all people. You need to read.[8]

Certainly the Apostle Paul took very seriously his need to know. Yet, he was inspired by God in a way we are not.

John Wesley, in a letter to his niece Sarah, in a time not known for putting a premium on education for women, showed serious concern for the Christian's need for knowledge. After giving specific suggestions for Sarah to read and study the Bible, history, poetry, grammar, arithmetic, geography, logic, natural philosophy, metaphysics, and theology for at least five hours a day, he says: "by this course of study, you may gain all the knowledge which any reasonable Christian needs." He then admonishes her to remember that above all her great need is "to know the only true God, and Jesus Christ whom he hath sent."[9]

This great need to know is never satisfied for the Christian, Wesley's ambitious program for his niece would have taken a lifetime. It was probably meant to do just that. This idealistic goal is never reached, but this does not lessen our responsibility to it. The important thing is that one is on the road to fulfillment

I should say just a word about evangelistic methodology, or how to win souls, for those who are so concerned with practical matters. In my opinion any method of soul winning may be used that does not contradict the message of the gospel. I think there are many rather subtle methods of evangelism being used today that actually contradict the gospel and hence cause incredible harm.

---

[8]Charles H. Spurgeon, *Commenting and Commentaries* (London: Sheldon, 1876), p. 62.
[9]L. Tyerman, *The Life and Time of the Rev. John Wesley*, vol. 3 (New York: Harper, 1872), p. 359.

There is no question in my mind that evangelism needs to be serious business for the Christian and that the most effective methods are defined in the terms "relationship evangelism" or "lifestyle evangelism." We cannot discharge our duty by *only* giving a tract and then forgetting them. We must love the lost sinners, though not the sin, enough that we are willing to befriend them. We must be willing to patiently love them as our Lord patiently loved us. There are many practical things that could be said about evangelism methods that work and honor God, many of which are said in the books listed in the section in the bibliography on evangelism at the end of this book.

You and I will not win the world, but we can win (that is the Holy Spirit through us) individuals. In the youth group of one church I served, I had each active member write down the names of *two persons* they knew and loved who needed to know the Lord. Then I had them list everything they knew about those two people: their likes, dislikes, strengths, weaknesses, where they went, what they did. We then spent much time praying specifically for them and working with them intimately to help bring them to Christ. Within one year all the people on the list, with the exception of two, had accepted Jesus as their Lord and Savior. Praise God!

Sometimes we forget, or have never realized, there are rather obvious little practical things that can be done to win specific people. We are so confused about our responsibility to win the world that we get lost in the task. The most winnable people are our family and friends, if we patiently love and accept them as Christ accepted us, and show them Christ in us by witnessing with compassion, integrity and intelligence. Of course, we must be genuine ourselves. Someone has jokingly defined family and friends as "people who know us and love us anyway," but this cannot be our definition if we are to be effective ambassadors for Christ.

Robert Kennedy once said (copying from George Bernard Shaw), "Some men see things as they are and say, 'Why?' I dream things that never were and say, 'Why not?' " Knowledge of the Word and world are weights on a balance beam that keep a Christian upright on his way. Because I realize what the New Testament teaches about the Christian's need to know, and I believe all things are possible through Him, I share in love for Christ, hope for the world, and the vision for a knowledgeable church!

7 Free to Love the Unlovely

In any generation, if we as Christians, are to lead and/or impact the society in which we live, we must be willing to: (1) Be radically committed to God. Christians must realize their self-worth and very being come from knowledge and experience of God. And (2) we must form intimate communities in which we live in loving relation to one another and not as individuals caught up in personal priorities, prejudice, or petty ego.

–*Reflections*, Vol. II

If the mark of a human being is the ability to reason, to engage in abstract thought (for this is what it means to be created in God's image), then inseparably related is the ability to love. Yes, in the final analysis we are human, and marked by God's image, because we can (must) think and love. These two inseparable gifts are God's greatest to us. Indeed the ultimate sin for a person is to use these two gifts selfishly, or for only personal gain or personal fulfillment. Phil. 3:17-20 tells us:

> Brethren, join in following my example, and observe those who walk according to the pattern you have in us. For many walk, of whom I often told you, and now tell you even weeping, that they are enemies of the cross of Christ, whose end is destruction, whose god is their appetite, and whose glory is in their shame, who set their minds on earthly things.

I do not say, nor do I believe, that a person can earn his salvation (Eph. 2:8, 9) or study himself into heaven. Yet, Christianity is a religion of the mind. The *real* purpose for learning in the Christian faith is to honor God, to learn as much of His truth as is humanly possible, to share it in love with as many people as is possible. Another letter I received from a former student expresses this need:

> I lived in the protective shell of Christendom almost isolated from the reality of a lost and lonely world. Then I had the opportunity in the summer of '86 to work for a very prestigious engineering firm in Miami, Florida. I worked this summer with some very ambitious and intelligent people. People we would consider very well educated. In the materialistic eyes of our world they seemed to be financially stable and successful. In reality they were not.
> My faith was really challenged; for the first time in my life I realized that just telling people that I was a Christian was not enough. . . . I learned that for them to be able to process what I was telling them *they had to see the love of Christ in me, had to see me live it. I also had to be able to logically defend what I believed.* It was not enough for me to just know what I believed, but why I so strongly believed it.

Christian Love Is More than Humanistic

We have already said some things about love and knowledge (Phil. 1:9-11). Knowledge is a prerequisite to love, the very ground of love. Knowledge is necessary for love to grow, to flower in its fullness. Another aspect of being created in God's image is that human existence can have meaning. We are not just a collection of chemicals, electrical responses, and matter that came into existence by a long intricate process and then evolved the aspects of mind and consciousness (casually determined beings). Christians believe all life comes from God. Man, though, has some special marks in the very image of God that other life does not have. God designed humans to be what we are: thinkers, artists, lovers, builders; above all, worshipers. Our enormous creative capacity comes from our Creator.

Being in God's image, the abilities to think and to love, means that a person's life has both meaning and purpose. For the Christian, the meaning of life is love — service to God and our fellowman. Every one of us is uniquely loved by God and all are valued equally in His sight. We can enter into communion with God. For the Christian, our ability to love is a response to God's love for us. "In this is love, not that we loved God, but that He loved us and sent His Son to be the propitiation for our sins. Beloved, if God so loved us, we also ought to love one another" (1 John 4:10, 11). But with this privilege comes a great responsibility. People can find God's love only by constantly encountering Him through us as we experience God's love and share its richness with others.

The purpose of life for the Christian is therefore service. The Christian seeks to serve God with all his motives, words, and actions. All of life is seen as noble, because it is all serving God. When all of life is seen as God's service, pleasures gain in richness, and sorrow is carried with more stability. Certainly, knowledge is absolutely essential in this process, both knowledge of God and of the world.

Serving God involves service to mankind. The one includes the other. A man "cannot love God, whom he has not seen, if he does not love his brother, whom he has seen" (1 John 4:20). As God shared with us, we have the responsibility to share with others both in and outside the church.

Yet, we are not talking about just a "humanism" here.[1] "Secular humanism" may be defined as any philosophy which makes man the measure of all things and views man as the supreme force in the universe. In 1933 thirty-four American humanists, among them John Dewey, Edwin A. Burtt, and R. Lester Mondale,[2] made a declaration that put forth the fundamental principles of their philosophy in "Humanist Manifesto I." Norman L. Geisler says of that declaration:

> "Humanist Manifesto I" can be summarized as (1) atheistic regarding the existence of God, (2) naturalistic regarding the possibility of miracles, (3) evolutionistic concerning man's origin, (4) relativistic concerning values, (6) optimistic about the future, (6) socialistic in political view, (7) religious in attitude toward life, and (8) humanistic with regard to the methods which it suggests to those who would achieve its goals.[3]

---

[1] For an excellent treatment of what it is to be human see T.M. Kitwood, *What is Human?* (Downers Grove, IL: InterVarsity, 1977).

[2] John Dewey was an American pragmatist who is considered by many to be one of the fathers of modern education. Edwin A. Burtt was a very famous philosopher. R. Lester Mondale was a Unitarian minister and brother of Walter Mondale, former vice-president of the United States.

[3] Norman L. Geisler, *Is Man the Measure? An Evaluation of Contemporary Humanism* (Grand Rapids, MI: Baker Book House, 1983), p. 114.

In 1973 another group of humanists came together to update the statement made forty years before. They realized that the earlier statement was far too optimistic. This "Humanist Manifesto II" was signed by such notables as Isaac Asimov, Brand Blanshard, Antony G. N. Flew, A. J. Ayer, B. F. Skinner, Joseph Fletcher, and Jacques Monod.[4] They continued "with earlier humanists in affirming that God, prayer, salvation, and providence are part of 'an unproved and outmoded faith.'"[5]

A third statement, "A Secular Humanist Declaration," appeared in 1980, signed by many who had signed the 1973 statement. It may seem surprising that this statement was drafted so soon after the 1973 one, but the most important aspects of this third statement are those in which it differs from the earlier two:

> First, of all, these secular humanists wish to be called democratic secular humanists. The stress on democracy is evident throughout. Second, nowhere do they claim to be religious humanists as do the authors of prior manifestos. This is particularly strange, since humanists have pleaded for recognition as a religious group and since humanism has even been defined as a religion by the United States Supreme Court (Torcaso v. Watkins, 1961). Indeed, the declaration could be justly characterized as antireligious, for it particularly attacks the recent trend toward more conservative religious beliefs. The bulk of the declaration, in fact, seems to be a reaction against recent trends contrary to secular humanism. Finally, one cannot help but notice a strange inconsistency in that the declaration affirms academic freedom and yet insists that scientific creationism not be allowed in public-school science classes (see p. 93, n.9.).[6]

This third statement certainly stresses, as did the ones that came before it, naturalism, evolutionism, and man's ability to

---

[4]Isaac Asimov is a very famous writer of science fiction. Brand Blanshard is a famous philosopher. A. J. Ayer and Antony Flew are philosophers who are perhaps the most famous representatives of philosophical atheism. B. F. Skinner is a famous psychologist and educational theorist. Joseph Fletcher is a well-known situational ethicist. Jacques Monod is a well-known biologist.
[5]Geisler, p. 115.
[6]*Ibid.*, p. 121.

save himself, a subtle self-love.

Christians believe that the most effective and selfless service is given to other humans when it is seen as part of the service to God. Love and knowledge are not only inseparably related to each other, but also to the very meaning and purpose of life. The difference between a Christian's need to know and the secular humanist's is this: For the Christian, knowledge is essential to understand reality as God created it; to understand special revelation, the Bible, which He has given us; to understand the facts of and to defend the truth of Christianity in order to share God's love with others. But knowledge is never an end in itself or something to be worshiped for its own sake. Biblical faith is rational, but it cannot fall into a false humanism that worships the creation rather than the Creator.

Secular humanism is evil. It puts man in God's place. Perhaps it is the ultimate evil, because it puts man in a place to be worshiped and in the process denies the very nature and essence of man created in *God's image*. In fact, it ultimately demeans man, makes him less than he really is. But a word of caution is appropriate here. While secular humanism is definitely a powerful force in our society, it is by no means the only, or even the dominant force. We Christians must be careful not to paint with too wide a brush. Sometimes well-meaning Christians, in their oversimplification and misunderstanding, zealously contribute more to the problem than to the solution.

For example, I support Christian education, but to say that our public schools in America are controlled by secular humanists becomes little more than a self-fulfilling prophecy. When Christians assign the public schools to Satan, then we help in large measure to give them to Satan in fact. The truth is that there are many thousands of dedicated Christians who are teaching and administering in many, if not most, public schools in all states. We should support them and help them to be the salt, light and leaven as they are already functioning. But when we make untrue generalizations that really say *all* of our public schools are controlled by the secular humanists, we only undercut these Christians who labor valiantly in a field where Christians must not, cannot give in to the forces of evil. And we often make them feel inferior or depressed because we are giving the wrong message in our sweeping generalization.

We should support them in several ways: by actively praying for them, their ministry and our public schools daily; by giving them the recognition that they deserve; by being actively involved in our public schools (attending school board meetings, being members of advisory committees to public school boards, contributing good books that are tastefully done and teach Christian values to public school libraries); by having classes in our churches for members who are public school teachers and workers so that they can share their experiences and learn how to integrate their faith with their job; and by some of us having our children in public schools so that our children can minister to the children of unbelievers. (This, of course, assumes that some of our churches and families are training children so that they *can* minister.)

Christian Love, Like Knowledge, Comes from God

In English, we have only one word to express all kinds of love, but Greek has no fewer than four: *eros*, used mainly for love between the sexes; *storge*, which has to do with family affection; *philia*, which is the commonest word for love in the Greek language and means to look on someone with affectionate regard, friendship. (This is the word for the love of husband and wife); *philein* is best translated to *cherish*. *Agape* (noun) and *agapan* (verb) are by far the commonest New Testament words for love, and means a pure, giving, sacrificial love.

Love is the greatest of all virtues, the characteristic virtue of the Christian faith. It would not be true to say that the New Testament only uses *agape* or *agapan* to express Christian love. A few times *philein* is used (John 5:20, 16:27; 1 Cor. 16:22), but *agape* is used almost 120 times in the New Testament and *agapan* more than 130 times. Christian love — *agape* — must not only extend to our nearest and dearest, our kin, our friends and those who love us; Christian love must extend to the Christian fellowship, to our neighbor, to our enemy, to all the world.

The other words for love are words which express primarily emotion and have to do with the affairs of the heart. *Agape* has to do with the mind. It is far more than an emotion. It is a principle by which we intentionally live. *Agape* has supremely to do with the wIL It can perhaps be best defined as: "intelligently, intensely willing the best for another."

This *agape*, this Christian love, is not merely an emotional experience; it is a deliberate principle of the mind. It can come only from God, through Christ. It is available only to Christians (Gal. 5:22; Rom. 15:30; Col. 1:8.) It is the power to love the unlovable. It demands, not that we cherish our enemies in the same way we love those closest to us, but that we should have at all times a certain attitude of the mind. In Matt. 5:43-48, we are told to love our enemies so that we would be like God, sons of our Father who is in heaven. I wish it were practiced more in churches that claim to be Christian.

The New Testament tells us much about God's love for us. Love is the *very nature* of God (1 John 4:7, 8; 2 Cor. 13:11). God's love is *universal* (John 3:16), It is *sacrificial* love; He gave His Son for us (1 John 4:9, 10; John 3:16). God's love is *undeserved* by us (Rom. 5:8; 1 John 3:1; 4:9, 10). It is a *merciful* love (Eph. 2:4). God's love is a *saving* and a *sanctifying* love (2 Thess. 2:13). It is a *strengthening* love (Rom. 8:37). God's love is an *inseparable* love (Rom. 8:39). It is a *rewarding* love (James 1:12; 2:5). God's love is a *chastening* love (Heb. 12:6).

The New Testament also tells us what the characteristics of Christian love are. Christian love is *sincere* (Rom. 12:9; 2 Cor. 6:6; 8:8; 1 Pet. 1:22). It is *innocent;* it never willfully injures another (Rom. 13:10). Christian love is *generous* (2 Cor. 8:24). It is a love that is *practical,* issues in action (Heb. 6:10; 1 John 3:18). Christian love is *forbearing* (Eph. 4:2). It issues in *forgiveness* and *restoration* (2 Cor. 2:8). Christian love is not *sentimental;* it does not shut its eyes to the faults of others (2 Cor. 2:4). It *controls liberty* (Gal. 5:13; Rom. 14:15). Christian love *controls truth;* it is never cruel or unsympathetic, never attempts to hurt (Eph. 4:15). It is *the bond which holds Christian fellowship together* (Phil. 2:2; Col. 2:2). Christian love is the power *in the perfecting of the Christian life* (Rom. 13:10; Col. 3:14; 1 Tim. 1:5, 6:11; 1 John 4:12). Certainly, we can love only because we are created in God's image.

For the Christian the twin abilities — the ability to think and to love — give us meaning and purpose in life. This gift of God's love within us must be used to glorify God and witness to men. Christian love must issue in service, both to God and to our fellowman.

8 The Holy Spirit and Knowledge

More than a spirit of unity, we should seek a unity of Spirit!
—*Reflections*, Vol. II

The role of the Holy Spirit in the life of the believer, and His relationship to knowledge, has been neglected almost entirely by some Christians, seriously abused by others. I must say with great conviction that I do not want to be guilty of either mistake.

It is very important in this discussion to realize that the Holy Spirit is part of the Godhead, the very essence of God. Theologians refer to the Holy Spirit as the third person of the Holy Trinity. Because the Holy Spirit is very God as is the Son and the Father, He cannot contradict himself or what He has revealed in His revelation to us, the Bible. Thus, every claim regarding what the Holy Spirit does and how He works must be judged according to the teaching of Scripture. Whatever is claimed as "from the Holy Spirit" cannot disagree with what He himself has written and must be judged by this standard.

I want to be quick to add that I do not want to limit the Holy Spirit in any possible way. He can be limited only by His nature and by what He himself has told us in the Bible about how He will or will not function. I am very sure that systematic theologians need to do more work in developing an adequate doctrine of the Holy Spirit. This must be done.

Logic — that is, correct reasoning and the principles of correct reasoning — comes from the very nature of God. God created man in His image and gave us language so that we could think His own thoughts after Him. Obviously there cannot be any contradiction or division between the Holy Spirit and the Christian's need to know. Because the Holy Spirit is one part of the very essence of God, He will function in every way according to the character of God as revealed by Jesus and the Bible. This realization is of great importance in developing a doctrine of the Holy Spirit.

The Holy Spirit in Scripture

The Holy Spirit is called by many names in the Scripture. Among His names are: "Spirit of Christ" (1 Pet. 1:2; Phil. 1:19), and "the Comforter" (*Parakletos* is one called alongside to help, i.e., *Intercessor* — John 14:26, 15:2e). In John 14:26 we are 'told: "But the Helper, the Holy Spirit, whom the Father will send in My name, He will teach you all things, and bring to your remembrance all that I said to you." It is clear in the context of the Scripture here that this is a promise to the apostles that they will be inspired to remember and write correctly the Scriptures. The symbols of breath, wind, a dove, the finger of God and fire are used for the Holy Spirit. We are told "it is the Spirit who bears witness, because the Spirit is the truth" (1 John 5:7), that Jesus is the Christ.

In the Old Testament there seemed to be five aspects to the work of the Holy Spirit: He was at work in creation and in making man (Gen. 1:2 and 2:7); He seemed to equip people for special jobs (Ex. 31:3; Judg. 3:10, 14:6); the Spirit was at work inspiring the prophets (Num. 11:29; Isa. 73:10, 11); even in the Old Testament, the Holy Spirit seemed to have worked in moral living (Ps. 51 and 139); the Holy Spirit was to foretell the Messiah (Isa. 11:2-9; 42:1-4; 61:1, 2).

In the New Testament, the Holy Spirit also worked to inspire the Scriptures (John 14:26). In 2 Pet. 1:21, we are told: "For no prophecy was ever made by an act of human will, but men moved by the Holy Spirit spoke from God." A major work of the Holy Spirit in the New Testament was in the life of Christ in His virgin conception (Matt. 1:20, 25) and setting Jesus apart for His ministry (Matt. 3:16, 17). As Jesus was conceived of the Holy Spirit, so His whole life, work and ministry was in the power of the Spirit. He was led by the Spirit into the wilderness (Matt. 4:1). Geoffrey W. Bromiley writes:

> In sum, Christology is no less ineffectual than inconceivable without pneumatology, whether at the level of the "for us" or

that of the "in us." Both are equally unthinkable, of course, without "Patrology," if we may so use the word. One cannot abstract Son from Spirit, or Spirit from Son, or both from Father. The work of revelation and reconciliation is the work of the triune Godhead therein reconciling and revealed.[1]

The Holy Spirit Works in the Lives of Men

The Holy Spirit works in the world to convict the world of sin, in the lives of both unbelievers and believers. In John 16:7-11, we are told:

> But I tell you the truth, it is to your advantage that I go away; for if I do not go away, the Helper shall not come to you; but if I go, I will send Him to you. And He, when He comes, will convict the world concerning sin, and righteousness, and judgment; concerning sin, because they do not believe in Me; and concerning righteousness, because I go to the Father, and you no longer behold Me; and concerning judgment, because the ruler of this world has been judged.

Because Jesus will no longer be in physical contact with us, the Holy Spirit will convict believers in regard to righteousness. And because Satan has been defeated in the death and resurrection of our Lord, the Holy Spirit will convict the world of judgment.

The Holy Spirit works in the process of conversion. We read in Titus 3:4-7:

> But when the kindness of God our Savior and His love for mankind appeared, He saved us, not on the basis of deeds which we have done in righteousness, but according to His mercy, by the washing of regeneration and renewing by the Holy Spirit, whom He poured out upon us richly through Jesus Christ our Savior, that being justified by His grace we might be made heirs according to the hope of eternal life.

The Holy Spirit is an agency in turning men from darkness to light, and from the power of Satan to God.

But how is it that the Spirit operates on the minds and

---

[1] Geoffrey W. Bromiley, *The Holy Spirit*, originally published as the thirteenth and final in a series of essays on "Fundamentals of the Faith" in *Christianity Today*.

hearts of men? We must not limit the power of the Holy Spirit nor ignore human agency (man's ability) and human responsibility. It must be obvious that the Holy Spirit does not exercise coercive power over the mind of man. This would be to force salvation on us. This God does not do.

Certainly I believe that the Holy Spirit is always working in the world (though sometimes things look pretty dark), to exercise a providential influence over the world. I do not think that this is at odds with human freedom, but somehow — I may not, nor may anyone else know the exact details — there is a providence, the Holy Spirit, at work in all our world. This working seems to help people be receptive to the Word, but it does not replace the need for hearing the message of the gospel.

Without question the Holy Spirit operates on the minds and emotions of men in order to bring about their conversion through the Word of God (Ps. 19:7). In Luke 8:4-15, Jesus himself, in explaining a parable, says — the Word of God is like seed sown (v. 11). The Word, the message of the gospel which was given by Jesus and inspired in written form by the Holy Spirit, is used by the Holy Spirit to bring about conversion and the fruits of the Spirit (Gal. 5:22-26). Paul says, "For I am not ashamed of the gospel, for it is the power of God for salvation to everyone who believes" (Rom. 1:16). In 1 Cor. 4:15, Paul tells us, "In Christ Jesus I became your father through the gospel." But the Spirit is the author of the gospel. In 1 Pet. 1:23, we are told that we are born of imperishable seed, "through the living and abiding word of God" (see also John 3:5 and 1 John 3:9). Thus it is certain that the Holy Spirit uses the Word of God, the message of salvation in the Bible, to convert men.

The Holy Spirit also works in the lives of believers (Acts 2:38) as a comforter (John 16:26). The Holy Spirit had to be given after Jesus had been glorified (John 7:37-39). Rom. 5:5 tells us that "the love of God has been poured out within our hearts through the Holy Spirit who was given to us" (see also 1 Cor. 6:11; 2 Cor. 1:22; Rom. 8:9-11; Gal. 4:6, and Eph. 4:30.) The Holy Spirit dwells in us and "helps our weakness; for we do not know how to pray as we should, but the Spirit

Himself intercedes for us with groanings too deep for words" (Rom. 8:26). The Holy Spirit works in the life of the believer to strengthen the inner man (Eph. 3:16) so that we may become partakers of the divine nature.

The Holy Spirit, the Scripture, and Knowledge

1 John 2:27 reads: "And as for you, the anointing which you received from Him abides in you, and you have no need for anyone to teach you; but as His anointing teaches you about all things, and is true and is not a lie, and just as it has taught you, abide in Him."

Some people have misused this passage. It is certainly not supporting any kind of "spiritual mysticism" whereby the Holy Spirit will give you knowledge apart from or contradictory to the Scripture. Nor does it teach that knowledge is unimportant, or that we do not need to be taught. John states plainly in verse 26 that this is a test to be used on false teachers: "These things I have written to you concerning those who are trying to deceive you." It is clear from verse 27 that they do not need to listen to these false teachers because they have been taught the Word of God by Jesus and the apostles. And they have the indwelling of the Holy Spirit who will give them assurance (Rom. 8:16).

We know that however the Holy Spirit may communicate with us in His divinity and freedom, He bears witness to the truth, and the truth has been revealed through Jesus and recorded by the Holy Spirit in the Scriptures. This means, of course, if this "word from the Spirit" you think you have been given is not consistent with the clear teachings of Scripture, it is not a word from the Spirit. Further, one must wonder why it is necessary if this word is already in Scripture (as it must be, for surely all Christians believe that God has given us all that we need to know in Scripture for salvation and holy living). Is it fair to think that the Holy Spirit will in some way give us some knowledge that is already available in the Scripture to excuse our ignorance or laziness when the very purpose of Scripture was to reveal God's will clearly once and for all to us all?

I certainly do not know all the ways the Holy Spirit works,

but I do not recommend the pursuit of mysticism on our parts. And further, I do know that while I do not want to tell anyone what the Holy Spirit can and cannot do, I am clear that the Holy Spirit is not against knowledge, reason, or wisdom, and that what we claim about the Holy Spirit must be tested according to the best exegesis of Scripture possible.

In areas regarding the gifts of the Holy Spirit there is great controversy about a necessary "second work of grace," and the gift of speaking in tongues as a necessary sign of the indwelling of the Holy Spirit. (Even charismatics disagree here.) Though there is obviously much dispute in the Christian family regarding certain gifts — tongues and healing for example — it is also obvious that they must be practiced according to the dictates of the Bible (1 Cor. 14:1-33). I, for one, am not willing to divorce the work of the Holy Spirit from the Scripture and our understanding of it.

How does the Holy Spirit relate to knowledge? Very simply, all truth and genuine knowledge comes from God. Because God's very essence is rational and He created the universe in an orderly manner and man with reason, the Holy Spirit also uses reason to work within man. The prime tool of the Holy Spirit is His written word, the Bible. This is a very important theological and practical insight. In essence it says that we should not, cannot expect the Holy Spirit to work in ways other than those ordered by the Godhead.

It is essential to realize the place of the Holy Spirit in our doctrine of the Scripture. The Holy Spirit had a responsibility to inspire the writing of Scripture. We have a responsibility to study it and understand the objective truth recorded therein, and to live what it commands! We are misunderstanding the very purpose of God in giving us the Scriptures if we think that it is the Holy Spirit's place to somehow "make up for" or "cover" for our responsibility to study the very word He has given us. Studying the Bible is how we are told that we may know, understand and grow closer to our God.

Let us be very careful that, in developing a doctrine of the Holy Spirit, we do not make Him less than He is by thinking we can use Him in ways that the Godhead did not intend. Let us also be careful not to limit the power of the Holy Spirit by telling God how He must work apart from a clear understanding of what He himself has revealed in His Word. And most important, let us grant each other the right — because God himself has given it to each of us — to seek out God and His Holy Spirit in ways that are acceptable to Him, and not be too quick to condemn before we understand each other and study the Scriptures together. To God be the glory!

9 Renewing the Mind: Key to Christian Living

Only the trained mind can unlock the secrets of the Universe and truly think God's thoughts after Him!
–Reflections, Vol. III

One of the great problems with many churches, as noted, is that, for some reason or other, the preaching and teaching does not often translate to the everyday lives of church members. Churchmen do not readily understand how to take the content of the preaching/teaching and apply it to their lives at home, at work, at play. I think there are many reasons for this. Certainly one would have to examine the preaching and teaching itself to see if and where it was at fault.

It is also true that many Christians I have known were not visibly progressing toward Christian maturity. I believe there are two primary reasons for this: Most church members have not really confronted the real meaning and fullness of the gospel either (1) intellectually or (2) emotionally. In other words, most church members are not willing to be involved in the life of the church to the extent that serious disciplined study and deep emotional sharing take place. And most have not really experienced the emotional fullness of the words, "For God so loved the world that He gave His only begotten Son, that whoever believes in Him should not perish, but have eternal life" (John 3:16), in their own lives. Any Christian who has experienced the fullness of these words cannot simply fill a pew!

In Phil. 4:4-9, as Paul turns to his last series of admonitions to the Philippian church, he gives us an informal summary of the whole philosophy and spirit and conduct of the Christian life. Here Paul gives us a key, perhaps *the* key to Christian living.

Rejoice in the Lord Always

First Paul says, "Rejoice in the Lord always; again I will say, rejoice!" This has been called the "keynote" or the fundamental idea of the whole book of Philippians by many scholars (check 1:4, 1:18, 2:17, 18, 3:1 for example). It expresses the prevailing mood of Paul's own life. The man who sounded the stirring challenge, "rejoice in the Lord," was a prisoner bound by a chain to his guard, poor and lonely and in danger of death, yet triumphant and glad in the fellowship and service of Christ. This phrase also proclaims what God intended, the ideal for every follower of Christ. Paul insists that joy is not to be an occasional experience, intended only for exceptional people. This constant rejoicing is meant for *all* who name the name of Christ.

If you read this passage carefully, you can almost hear Paul thinking. A picture flashes in his mind not only of his own hardships but of all that is possible in the future — dark days, dangers and persecutions, times of pain as well as of pleasure. So Paul seems to say, "I know what I am saying. I have thought of everything that can possibly happen. I have experienced it, and still I say it — *rejoice!*" But we must remember the essential words, "in the Lord." Abiding joy, the kind Paul is talking about, is possible only in view of all a person has and may have because of his relationship to the Lord Jesus Christ.

Yet to the modern skeptic, we who are supposedly so with it and so well informed, this seems almost silly, at best extremely idealistic. But as we will see very shortly, Paul does not just give a strong idealistic statement here; he unlocks the key to its possibility. "In the Lord" we have peace with God.

"In the Lord" we have victory over temptation. "In the Lord" we have companionship in trial. And "in the Lord" we have assured hope for the life to come. Why are we so skeptical about the possibility of constant rejoicing? Why is it so hard for us to "rejoice always"? One cause of a lack of joy is the memory of past failure and faults. Added to regret and self-reproach and remorse there is the haunting fear of coming defeat. We are slow to believe in divine forgiveness, or to expect victory where once we have been overcome.

But as Christians the recollection of the past should make us humble in the present and guard us against self-confidence in the future; but if we believe anything, we surely should believe in the pardoning love of God and in the power which makes us "more than conquerors" in Christ. We must remember Phil. 4:13: "I can do all things through Christ who strengthens me." (Perhaps better remembered as "He, by His strength, can do all things in my life." Even here the emphasis must be on Him, not on us!)

Some people have a genius for gladness. There was a woman in one of the churches I served who was that way. She was always joyous, almost always singing inside. Others are continually inclined to take dark views of life. Their humor is seldom cheerful. They are almost proud to be pessimists. I have experienced church members like this also.

It is well to remember that dispositions may be controlled and cultivated. Here the help of our Lord is indispensable. The fruit of the Spirit is . . . joy. It is the very glory of a Christian that he is superior to his surroundings and can be radiantly cheerful even in times of great trial and distress. Christians must be in touch with reality. Yet, Christians need not let dark realities master or blind them to the radiance that comes from knowing Christ.

Let Your Forbearing Spirit Be Known

Joy is closely related to what we call gentleness. One whose own heart is ever singing will not usually be harsh or ungracious toward his fellow humans. Thus the exhortation to rejoice is followed by the admonition, "Let your gentleness" (as some versions say, "your forbearing spirit") "be known to all men." Possibly the best phrase to translate the Greek here is "sweet reasonableness." It is the opposite of stubbornly claiming your own selfish rights.

This word refers to something better than justice. It is the quality of *compassionate* justice, which comes into play when a person knows when not to apply the "letter of the law." Surely we, in our day, must be just, but lovingly, compassionately just. Of course the hard task is to show this sweet reasonableness toward the perverse, the thankless, and the unkind.

Don't Be Anxious, but Pray

Certainly we can take *everything* to God in prayer. There is nothing too great for God's power; and nothing too small for His fatherly care. Paul is saying that the cure for anxiety can he found in *believing prayer.*

In my experience as an ordained minister, having served several churches, I must say that one of the real problems with many Christians is that they do not seem to have real confidence in prayer. How strange for Christians! In my experience this is precisely because they are not really educated in their Christian belief.

They do not seem to really believe that if they sincerely pray with faith — trusting in God because of who He is and the evidence we have of His reliability in Scripture — that He will take care of the problem. They do not seem to really believe that when we give the problem over to Him, we can have a peace about it. Often this "believing," or reasonable trust, is essential as a basis for a psychological condition which itself will help in the answer; it removes the anxiety, which in turn often allows the person to take clear action based on an intelligent understanding of Scripture and the counsel of good Christian friends. Phil. 4:6, in one modern version, reads: "Don't worry about anything; instead, pray about everything." Instead of worrying, we Christians are urged to find peace of heart by turning to God and trusting Him because we know Him and that He is faithful.

The Mind Must Be Properly Disciplined

Now, in Phil. 4:9, Paul reveals to us the essential element that makes all he has instructed us so far not only a possibility but a reality. The human mind will always set itself on something. Whether you realize it or not you are always thinking (even asleep you may be dreaming). Paul says if you want to really live the Christian life, then *you must think about things that are important.* Paul insists that we do our part by controlling our minds and thoughts. Because, if we do not control our thoughts and make them Christ-centered by thinking on positive and edifying thoughts, then someone or something else is most certainly controlling our minds. And we cannot grow in Christ if we are being controlled by another. What are these high thoughts? Paul tells us clearly what the categories are:

"Whatever things are true." That is everything in motive and conduct that corresponds to the divine ideal revealed in Christ. John 8:32 tells us to know the truth because it alone will make us free. In John 14:6, Jesus proclaims, "I am the way, and the truth and the life; no one comes to the Father, but through Me." Many things in this world are really nothing more than deception and illusion. But the word and life of Jesus is Truth itself — something to build on because it reveals the very character of God.

Here is a positive ethic that must be taught to Christians, especially Christian young people. All too often we give them a negative ethic, telling them constantly what not to do. Through this truth we have the glorious privilege to live out the very character of God one with another. Truth forms the basis for what we choose and what we do. It is the most positive of all foundations for ethics, because through it the very character of God is revealed to us in Jesus the Son. By His example and because His Spirit lives in us, we can be expressions of God's very character in this world of illusion and deception.

"Whatever things are noble and honorable." Those things that call forth love and holiness and grace. The word in the Greek, *semnos*, is difficult to translate. It describes that which has the dignity of holiness upon it.

"Whatever things are just, or right." God himself is righteous and He loves those who conform to His standards, those who act in accord with divine or moral law. There are those who set their minds on pleasure, comfort and easy ways. The Christian's thoughts are set on duty to God and duty to man.

"Whatever things are pure." The Greek word here, *hagnos*, has the general sense of innocence. Purity of thought and purpose is a precondition of purity in word and action. We were cleansed when we were brought into the presence of God and made fit for service. Eph. 5:1-4 tells us to "be imitators of God as beloved children; and walk in love" (v. 1). We are not to "let immorality or any impurity or greed even be named among you, as is proper among saints" (v. 3). Every Christian should be motivated to apply in his own life what is taught here.

"Whatever things are lovely." Moffatt translates "lovely" as "attractive." The Greek might be paraphrased, "that which calls forth love." Some minds are so set on evil things, vengeance and punishment that all they call forth is bitterness and fear. The mind of the Christian is disciplined so that it will be set on lovely things — kindness, sympathy, forbearance.

"Whatever is of good repute." This word, *euphemos*, literally means fair-speaking. William Barclay suggests that it might not be going too far to say that it describes the things which are fit for God to hear.

"If there is any excellence, virtue. If there is anything worthy of praise." Paul tells us to fill the mind with the things that are good and deserve praise . . . take account of them. Our minds *must* be made to dwell upon these high moral ideals, upon things honorable, just, pure, lovely. Such disciplined high thinking cannot fail to result in nobility of character and in worthy deeds in a Christian's life. For as a man thinks, so is he.

Nothing can be of more vital importance than a proper control of thought, for this allows us to grow in Christian knowledge, love and service. Yes, the objects on which we allow our minds habitually to dwell determine our acts, our career, our destiny.

This passage is the key to Christian living. Only when we are in control of our minds through Christ Jesus can we rejoice constantly. We must learn these things as Paul learned them. And as he taught others, we must teach others. "And the God of peace will be with you" or as some versions say, "And the peace of God shall be with you!"

10 "Agony": Key to Christian Victory

As the pilgrims drew near, they saw a man standing alone, with his sword in his hand, and his armor stained with blood. Greatheart stopped and asked him what had happened. The man was tall and strong, with a brave, handsome face....

"My name is Valiant," he answered, "and I am a pilgrim. Three men came down this lane and attacked me as I was passing. They said I might take my choice of three things, either to join them in robbing the King's pilgrims, or to go back to my own city, or to be put to death on this spot."

"What did you say to them?" asked Greatheart.

"I told them that I had always tried to be honest, and I certainly should not become a thief now; and that, as for my own city, I should not have left it if I had been happy there, but it was a bad place, and I had forsaken it forever. Then they asked me if I wished to lose my life, and I said my life was worth too much for me to give it up lightly, and they had no right to meddle with the King's servants in such a manner. So they drew their swords, and I drew mine, and we have been fighting for nearly three hours. They have wounded me, but I think I wounded them also...."

"That was a hard battle, three men to one" said Greatheart.

"Yes," replied Valiant; "but I know I was fighting against my King's enemies, and that gave me courage."

"Did you not cry for help? Some of the King's servants might have been near enough to hear you."

"I cried to the King Himself, and I am sure He answered me. I could not have fought so long in my own strength."

Greatheart smiled. "You are one of our King's true servants! Let me see your sword. Ah, yes, this is from the right armory!"

"It is a good sword," said Valiant. "No man who has so fine a weapon need be afraid, if he has learned how to use it skillfully."

"And you fought for three hours?" said Greatheart. "Were you not ready to faint with fatigue?"

"No, I fought until my sword clung to my hand, as if it were a part of my arm; but I think that made me feel stronger."[1]

The word *agony* is commonly thought to signify some extreme physical pain. The dictionary defines *agony* as very painful suffering, either physical or mental, or perhaps both. *Agony* is often used lightly in such expressions as: "My shoes hurt: I'm in *agony*." Or, "I have to do my homework sometime; I might as well get the *agony* over now."

In the New Testament the word is used very rarely, and never without special emphasis. By studying the very few passages in which *agony* appears, we can gain insight into several important biblical questions: What did Jesus experience in the Garden of Gethsemane? How powerful is Satan? How can Christians defeat evil? What does the apostle Paul tell us through this word about the nature of a Christian's prayer life? We can also learn about a very essential requirement of victory in Christian living!

Before these questions can be answered, the meaning of the Greek word *agony* must be understood.

The Meaning of "Agony"

The Greek word *agonia* is transliterated in our English Bibles, not translated. To "transliterate" is to bring a word from one language to another by representing the same sound in the letters of another alphabet. To "translate" is, of course, to express the meaning of a word or sentence originally written in one language correctly in another. Thus we have the same problem with *agony* that we do with *baptize*, for example. The Greek word *baptizo* means "to immerse." Simply to use the Greek word *agonia* does not tell us its meaning either in Greek or in English.

Kittel's *Theological Dictionary of the New Testament* says of *agonia* that this word is "much used in relation to the

---

[1]Helen L. Taylor, *Little Pilgrim's Progress*, [adapted from John Bunyan's (1628-1688) classic work]. (Chicago: Moody Press), pp. 236-237.

Greek stadium. It originally meant a place of contest, or stadium, then the contest itself (including litigation and debate), and finally any kind of conflict."

Agony came to have the meaning pictured in the following scene: Two gladiators are fighting to the death. They have fought long and hard. Each is bloody, battered and torn, and all but beaten. Suddenly one of the gladiators lands a blow and sends the other crashing to the ground. This gladiator raises his sword to split the head of his fallen opponent. Then, in that crucial fraction of a second, the fallen gladiator experiences the meaning of the Greek word *agony*. He rallies every bit of strength left in his "all but defeated body" to rise up and win!

We see in the above scene two extremely important aspects of *agony*. First, the fallen gladiator rallies the last ounce of his remaining strength. Second, he maintains in that moment a completely positive mental attitude. He summons all the strength he can muster not simply to *try* to win, but rather to *WIN!* He will win because he *must*. There is no room for doubt in his mind. There is only one way for him, the way of victory. Paul often uses military and athletic metaphors for the struggle of the Christian!

Thus the Greek word *agony* has two very important prongs to its meaning: (1) a rallying of all one's strength and (2) a completely positive mental attitude.

"Agony" in the New Testament

Under the shadow of the cross the battle to which Christians are called takes on a new dimension and seriousness. The New Testament writers not only take over the twofold meaning of *agony*, but they enrich it by relating how Jesus, God incarnate, becomes the gladiator who fights a cosmic battle with evil in the garden and on the cross for each of us, for all mankind. In the New Testament the concept of "agony" is enriched several ways:

(1) The goal of a life that honors God can be reached only with the full expenditure of all our energies, with a continual striving to be like Him. Certainly, we are not saved "as a result of works, that no one should boast" (Eph. 2:9). But this does not mean that we do not have a responsibility to consciously, continually strive to be Christlike (that is "like Jesus Christ, especially in character or spirit"). The process of sanctification is lifelong, but one in which we have a good share of the responsibility. After all, He was our example in all things. In Luke 13:24 are Jesus' words: "Strive to enter by the narrow door; for many, I tell you, will seek to enter and will not be able." In Philippians 2:12 we are told to continue to "work out [our] salvation with fear and trembling." The struggle for Christlike character allows of no indolence or indecision. Paul further relates that the work of spreading God's good news is more than the faithful daily doing of one's duty (1 Tim. 2:2). It is a passionate struggle and a constantly renewed concentration of forces to achieve the goal.

> We proclaim Him, admonishing every man and teaching every man with all wisdom, that we may present every man complete in Christ. And for this purpose also I labor, *striving* according to His power, which mightily works within me (Col. 1:28,29).

(2) The struggle for maturity in Christian living demands not only full exertion but also rigid denial.

> Do you not know that those who run in a race all run, but *only* one receives the prize? Run in such a way that you may win. And everyone who competes in the games exercises self-control in all things. They then do it to receive a perishable wreath, but we an imperishable (1 Cor. 9:24,25).

The final goal is so high and glorious above all others. We must be willing to set aside our self-centered needs and desires in order to fit ourselves for God's battle in the arena of life (1 Cor. 9:27).

Paul is here talking not about a contempt for the world, but rather about insight into life. "Better is the enemy of the best." Christians must strive for excellence to honor their Lord. In the Christian world, as an ugly mirror image of the real world, we seem to be satisfied with second best when, as Christians, we should be constantly striving for excellence. But what is Christian excellence. I have often heard that: "If it is Christian it should be a little bit better." Better in what sense? Better by the standards of the world? Better by the worldly standards of success, i.e., more money, more power, more, more, more. I think not! Our bottom line must not, cannot, be "nickels and numbers." We are called to faithfulness, not to success as the world views success!

The success ethic of twentieth century America stands clearly and forcefully in opposition to the Christian ethic. Unfortunately many Christians do not see this! We are judged as successful by what we *do*, not by who we *are*. We are judged to be "successes" by how much *money* we make, *power* we have, by what *others* think of us. But for Jesus "successful" is synonymous with being "faithful," to Him and our fellows; by *being* a certain way, not by *doing* anything as such! Now to be sure, *being* something means we will strive to act with integrity, i.e., with love, joy, peace, and so on (Gal. 5:22-23), but the "being" is the essential basis for the "doing."

I personally know of ministries that are run by the "nickels and numbers" syndrome. Whole ministries are *pervaded* by the "bigger is greater" success syndrome! Thank the Lord that many are seeing through this subtle evil. It is the "being" that *makes us* a success! The "doing," e.g., bigger numbers, more money, more, more, more *never* make us successes; any more than does the perceived lack of it in the eyes of others make us *failures*.

(3) The supreme goal for which Christ suffered and for which we suffer is the salvation of many — not just our own salvation. "The one stands for the many. All must stand for the one, mustering around him in a loyal fellowship of battle" (compare Col. 4:12, 13). This is the true meaning of community for the Christian. Paul often uses the imagery of Christians doing battle alongside

other Christians against the forces of evil. Just as we share our blessings we are to share the combat in this world.

Christ in the Garden

In the Garden of Gethsemane we see the Christ, King of the universe, Lord of lords, falling to His knees, "And being in *agony* He was praying very fervently; and His sweat became like drops of blood, falling down upon the ground" (Luke 22:44). Christ was pouring himself out in prayer. R. C. Foster, in *The Final Week*, says:

> The word translated "great drops of blood" can be rendered "blood clots." It seems to mean more than that His drops of sweat resembled drops of blood by their size and frequency; otherwise there would be no reason or force in such a comparison.

There does seem to be some precedent medically for a "bloody sweat." Foster further contends that even if there were no such medical phenomenon known to us it does not prove Christ did not sweat blood. His agony was unique.

Yet the text does say "like" drops of blood, not that the sweat was really blood. Either is possible, but what is important is the Lord here experienced an *agony* of the greatest intensity. The word itself indicates a "supreme concentration of powers in face of imminent decisions or disasters."

Satan, it seemed, was about to defeat the Creator and Sustainer of the universe. Jesus had been turned away so many times. Even His apostles did not understand the true nature of His kingdom. He went saddened and rejected to the garden. He felt all but beaten and He dropped to His knees to pray. This is when the gladiator Christ experienced the meaning of *agony*. He had been fighting a constant battle with Satan and it seemed that He was about to lose. Then in prayer He rallied all His strength — all the strength in the universe — with a positive mental attitude to *WIN!* He knew He had to defeat

"AGONY": KEY TO CHRISTIAN VICTORY

Satan for mankind to be redeemed. We see here not the fear of death, but Christ's "concern for victory in the face of the approaching decisive battle on which the fate of the world depends." Jesus rose from that agony a victorious Lord.

This tells us the power of Satan. Jesus, the Christ, had to rally all His power to withstand and finally defeat Satan. The Lord of the universe had to give His all; we Christians must not think that we can defeat evil with our own strength. Only with the strength of Jesus can we prevail as He did. We need His help! And, through Him each other's help.

Victory in Prayer

Paul said to the Romans (15:30): "Now I urge you, brethren, by our Lord Jesus Christ and by the love of the Spirit, to *strive* together with me in your prayers to God for me." Paul's *strive* uses the same root word we found in Luke 22:44. Here it means to combat in company with anyone; to exert one's strength with, to be earnest in aiding, to contend along with a fellow combatant. The world *strive* denotes intense agony or effort such as was used in the Greek games. Paul tells us to agonize with him in our prayers!

Again, we see the imagery of victory or death. We must rally all the strength available to us through Christ in a positive mental attitude in our prayer lives. We must experience agony in our prayer lives knowing that if we pray in the framework of the will of God our prayers will be answered. Christians, though at a distance from one another, may unite in their prayers. Yes, Christians *must* be "deadly" serious about their prayer lives!

The lessons we learn from the New Testament word *agony* are limited only by our human ability to understand and accept the will of God. Now we begin to imagine the power of Satan; what Jesus went through before going victoriously to the cross; what we must do to overcome sin and temptation. We must be vital in our prayer lives. We must study the Bible, the Word of God. We must not take the battle we wage with and for Christ lightly.

The Pilgrim's Progress

We started our "journey" into an understanding of "agony" with a quote from *Little Pilgrim's Progress*. Valiant knew much about "agony." Indeed he had just experienced it! All the elements are there: (1) His alternatives were surrender, death, or victory as a Christian. In our world there are many who will try to tempt us to "rob the King's pilgrims," that is to settle for second best and thereby cheat the church. Or, to get us to "stay in (our) own city," our old sinful life and therefore not be an effective witness to others in need in our world.

(2) Valiant had just gone through an intense conflict. He had fought for hours and had been wounded, but *not* beaten. He had also wounded them, but it had been "a hard battle." Ours will be as well! Just as Valiant took courage from the fact that he *knew* he was fighting his King's enemies so must we. (3) Valiant cried out to the "King Himself." This brings us back to "agony" in our prayer lives! And the King heard him: ". . . and I am sure He answered me. I could not have fought so long in my own strength." In the final analysis we must rely on His strength!

(4) Yet, Valiant had a part to do as well. He had to rally all his strength to *WIN!* Greatheart smiled and said: "You are one of our King's true servants! Let me see your sword. Ah, yes, this is from the right armory!" We must be armed with His armor (Eph. 6:10-24). "for our struggles is not against flesh and blood, but against the rulers . . . against the spiritual forces of wickedness in the heavenly places." We must:

> Stand firm therefore, HAVING GIRDED [our] LOINS WITH TRUTH, AND HAVING PUT ON THE BREASTPLATE OF RIGHTEOUSNESS, AND HAVING SHOD [our] feet with the preparation of the gospel of peace; in addition to all, taking up the shield of faith with which you will be able to extinguish all the flaming missiles of the evil one. And take THE

"AGONY": KEY TO CHRISTIAN VICTORY

HELMET OF SALVATION, and the sword of the Spirit, which is the word of God (emphasis added, vv. 14-17).

Notice that at least five of the parts of our armor (girded with *truth*, the breastplate of *righteousness*, shield of *faith*, the helmet of *salvation*, and sword, the *word of God*) involve in some way or another mental acts on the part of the believer!

And then, we are again told to have the most active prayer lives. Paul goes on to tell us: "With all prayer and petition pray at all times in the Spirit, and with this in view, be on the alert with all perseverance and petition for all the saints" (v.18).

(5) He had a completely positive mental attitude. " 'Let me see your sword. Ah, yes, this is from the right armory!' 'It is a good sword,' said Valiant. 'No man who has so fine a weapon *need be afraid, if he has learned how to use it skillfully.*'" [Emphasis added — again another mental act involved.] Our "sword" is the Bible, the Word of God. We must *learn* how to use it! We need not "be afraid" if we have learned how to use it properly! " 'Were you not ready to faint with fatigue?' 'No, I fought until my sword clung to my hand, as if it were a part of my arm; but I think that made me feel stronger.' " Our "sword," the Word of God and our knowledge of it, *must* become "second nature" to us! Yes, we can learn much from Valiant. There was no room for doubt in Valiant's mind. There is only one way for him, the way of victory. There can be only one way for us as well. The way of victory.

Indeed, Christ has *already* won the victory for us! "All" we have to do is to *discipline* ourselves in the spiritual life, in the knowledge of the Word, so that we can take advantage of the strength He can and will give us! But, as we all know, even this is not easy. It is not as if our salvation depends on the fight, but surely in a real sense that of others may. It takes consecrated worship, urgent prayer, real fellowship, and intense preparation (serious study) on our parts.

The simple truth — with very complex implications — is that every person, male or female, black or white, rich or poor, who claims to be a Christian has a *personal* responsibility to spend the rest of their lives as *serious students* of the text of Scripture!

Being Christians

"Being" Christians is far more basic than "doing" Christian things. Notice here I do not mean that "doing" Christian things/acts is not important. Yet, we — many, many in the church today — are caught in the success trap of twentieth century America! There must be an intensity and an integrity about our Christian lives. We *must* be *alive* as Christians, not just existing! The view of our Lord from the garden to the cross is a vision of victory that men might be brought back to God. Is the view of your life in Christ, from new birth to eternity, a vision of victory that others might have a chance to know Him?

And what of Valiant?

> The same messenger . . . summoned Valiant also, but he went over the river later in the day. He had no fear of the crossing, for he has always been brave, and his heart was full of trust in the good King.
> "Mine has been a hard pilgrimage," he said, "and I have had to fight my way through many troubles and dangers; but I am going now to my true home in the Celestial City, where I shall be safe and happy forever."
> The good soldier had no longer any use for his sword, so he left the bright weapon in Greatheart's care, and desired him to give it to some other pilgrim.[2]

Amen! May it be so of us as well!

---

[2]Taylor, *Little Pilgrim's Progress*, p. 255.

11 Beware of "One-eyed" Kings!

There is a disease consuming our world today:
A disease more insidious than materialism, more ravishing than cancer, more dangerous than bigotry, more infectious than racism.
That disease is MEDIOCRITY.
There is a real danger it will destroy our nation, emasculate the church, become a way of life for individual Christians. But it will never conquer the Gospel of Christ!
–Reflections, Vol. I

Perhaps you have heard the old saying: "The more things change the more they stay the same." I have heard many say that the church is in desperate need today, in a terrible condition. We all ask why and many of us have "our" answers. Recently, I heard it said the problem with the church is that individual Christians lack the power of the Holy Spirit. This is undoubtedly true. Of course, charismatics and non-charismatics will have a different opinion about just what constitutes the "power of the Holy Spirit."[1]

Clearly the Bible teaches that the Holy Spirit lives in the "heart" of every believer. So what is the problem? I think a large *part* of the problem is in a rather significant current day *mis*understanding of Christianity. Christians today do not understand the relationship between "faith" and "reason." Ironically, we are supposed to be the most educated generation which has ever lived (and in some ways we are), but Christians have more or less abdicated when it comes to real "knowledge," i.e., the ability to reason, to think critically or analytically. Just because the atheist world isn't much better off doesn't help us terribly!

---

[1] See chapter eight in this book: "The Holy Spirit and Knowledge."

The Situation in Today's Church

Even the churches' leaders, its "preachers" (some of the most famous) do not really understand the significance of the fact that Christianity is a religion based on propositional revelation (a revelation which is propositionally true[2]), i.e., *we cannot practice what we really do not understand!* And, we cannot avail ourselves of the power of the Holy Spirit if we will not understand! *Credo ut intelligam*: "I believe in order that I may know."

Why do I say that many of the most famous of today's preachers do not understand this? Because they have not been properly educated in the original languages of the Bible, theology, philosophy, logic, history, and other important disciplines. Remember what John Wesley said in the letter to his niece Sarah: "by this course of study, you may gain all the knowledge which *any reasonable Christian* needs"[3] [emphasis added]. Wesley was writing around two hundred years ago. Further, Wesley said that such study should consume at least five hours daily. If this were true then, just think *how much greater the need is today.*

The church universal does not need even ten flamboyant preachers who draw more attention to their personalities than to the person of Jesus. The average Christian, in the average church, is far too likely now to fix on the messenger, instead of internalizing the message. The church needs tens of thousands of ministers who are willing to be filled by the Holy Spirit. This is a lifelong process of maturing in knowledge and love of Christ. These are humble, patient human beings who will allow their characters to be transformed (Rom. 12:1-2, Phil. 1:9-11) so that Christ will live through them and be radiated to all who will see. To my knowledge, the greatest argument against empire building in the name of the church (like so many T.V. preachers have done) is the example of Jesus of Nazareth.

The church would be far better off if most of the television

---

[2] See the section on "The Nature of Propositional Revelation" in chapter four.
[3] See page 74.

preachers went off the air. Christianity might even be judged better, as having more credibility and integrity if this happened! (Thankfully many have.) Yet, many of the famous preachers of today speak and write authoritatively as if they knew everything when they have not paid the high price Wesley speaks of which is necessary for "any reasonable Christian." Some of the most famous television preachers do not even have accredited bachelors degrees, let alone bonafide seminary or graduate education. They have "authored" dozens of books, but they personally have not written a word! This is because they have people — referred to as "ghostwriters" — who write for them.

Others have accredited seminary education, but unfortunately from schools which present only a very narrow view. Church members should be very leery of listening to these "one-eyed kings." Certainly, they should be careful not to revere them or to consider them "experts" on anything — except perhaps empire building.

Even the best of today's radio "exegetical, expository preachers" are woefully inadequate in real knowledge and preparation, but are they well "marketed"! What bothers me is all these preachers who are writing on *anything* as if they were "experts" on *everything*, who don't even have the permit (degree) . . . or the knowledge it represents. Nationally famous "preachers" who have only Master of Divinity (M.Div.) degrees in terms of formal education, but who are called "doctor," have signed contracts with evangelical publishing houses with six figure advances to write commentaries on the whole Bible (or the New Testament). What makes these preachers think they have the expertise — or the right — to be presented to the church as such experts on the text of the Bible?[4]

One very well-known exegetical, expository radio preacher, who shall remain nameless (again, called "doctor" with only an M.Div.), has a staff of ten to twelve people writing his material for him. Realize that these empire builders in

---

[4]It would be helpful here to refer to Appendix A: "A View of Faith and Learning."

the name of Christ, with their demanding schedules and empires to manage — not to mention preaching — cannot possibly have the time to write, let alone the time to do the patient research necessary for real scholarship. (I remember one very good preacher — with no connection to the electronic media, who wrote good short books on popular subjects of spiritual interest — used to say that each of his books underwent at least 16 rewritings at his hand *before* they were submitted to the publisher.) Besides this staff of ten to twelve, an evangelical publishing house paid one editor (who worked outside the daily life of the company, but was paid totally by the press) $42,000.00 a year to edit only one book from this same radio preacher in every ten to twelve months! Again, guess who really did the writing?

Another famous Christian scholar (whom we might add is not by training a specialist in the original languages or the text of Scripture), "lucky" enough to have a study Bible named after him, has received between $320,000.00 and $400,000.00 (and more) a year for many years from this one project — all profit made off of the Bible! (And, it was a woefully inadequate study Bible to boot!) This whole *trend* — of Christian superstar authors who make hundreds of thousands of dollars, even millions — in Christian publishing is not only bad stewardship in the name of the church — it is shameful! The examples I have mentioned here are just the very small "tip" of a very large "iceberg" — I could give many more!

The present day condition of the church reminds me of an old French phrase: *au pays des aveugles les borgnes sont rois*, that is "in the country of the blind the one-eyed men are kings." This is certainly true in the church in our day. *Beware*, Christians! Help doesn't come from the blind and "one eye" doesn't give us the perspective nor the depth — remember one loses depth perception with only one eye — the church needs today to combat paganism, i.e., "naturalism," in all its hideous forms!

Alcuin's Example

Alcuin (c. A.D. 735-804) is to most of us an unknown figure in church history. Yet, he "was an accomplished poet, biographer, biblical commentator, and theologian. In addition, he published textbooks on grammar, rhetoric, and dialectics."⁵ He was fighting the same battle we are fighting. The church in Alcuin's day was very ignorant and was mixing all sorts of pagan rites with Christianity, even as we are mixing "pagan rites" — such as materialism, the gospel of health and wealth, the twentith century success syndrome — with Christianity!⁶

During this time, which is called the Dark Ages,

> the church in western Europe made a number of attempts to combat aspects of pagan practice that had seriously compromised Christianity.... On 21 April 742 a German council passed a decree condemning pagan rites that 'foolish men perform in the churches' — such as the sacrifice of animals, sacrifices to the dead, incantations, and divination.⁷

It may sound strange to relate the church of today to the church in the Dark Ages, but perhaps there are more similarities than we would really want to admit. It may be that the "pagan practices" and ideologies are much more "sophisticated," but just as pagan nevertheless.

Alcuin and Emperor Charlemagne (742-814) "understood that as long as great numbers of the clergy and the people were uneducated it would be impossible to root out paganism or to realize Augustine's vision of Christianization." So they "teamed up" to educate the people, establish schools, and build great libraries. Charlemagne and Alcuin working together "established a base for the recovery of classical learning. They began public education and fostered the common use of Latin as the language of educated discourse."⁸

In his *Epistola de litteris colendis* (784-785), Alcuin "insisted that orthodoxy (right faith) must be clothed in a form consistent with sound doctrine and conveyed in language that is universally understood."⁹ When Alcuin became the abbot of

---

⁵John D. Woodbridge, *Great Leaders of the Christian Church* (Chicago: Moody Press, 1988), pp. 121-126.
⁶More than three hundred of Alcuin's letters survive and they form a rich treasury of insight into his mind and that of his time.
⁷Woodbridge, *Great Leaders of the Christian Church*, p. 123.
⁸*Ibid.*, p. 121.
⁹*Ibid.*, p. 124.

the great abbey of St. Martin of Tours (796) at the invitation of Charlemagne, "he instituted a new curriculum. . . . He stressed the importance of grammatical structure in the study of Scripture and began programs for training monks and spiritual directors in *scriptural literacy*" (emphasis added). He also initiated a program "for the copying of great manuscripts, which was to be the source of splendid illuminations." Alcuin "gave new life to the liberal arts, with theology at their center."[10] He made a great contribution to the church and to the society of his day and did much which can serve as an excellent example for us today.

What brought civilization through the Dark Ages? "Why did we not have to start all over?"

> The reason is simple: Learning was kept alive by the Christian Church. In the monasteries, which were built like fortresses to keep out the ravaging barbarians, the monks were copying out books. The Bible and St. Augustine, but also histories and philosophy, Virgil and Cicero, texts of medicine and biology, poetry and engineering — all were copied out in longhand, read and discussed, preserved and stored for a more settled age to come which could use them. In the parish churches, the priest and those whom he would teach kept alive the art of reading, out of their devotion to the Word of God.[11]

Once again, it must be the church which will bring our world through our modern "dark ages." This can only be done if we meet the challenge of our day and age as others have met the challenge in their day and age. We need dozens of Christians like Alcuin and Charlemagne and, yes, C. S. Lewis for *today*, all working together with John 17 in mind to witness to the world of the truth and unity of the Christian faith.

"Education" is Only Part of the Answer:

Oh, there have been times when the church was more (or less) "educated!" There was a time when the best and the

---

[10]*Ibid.*, pp. 123, 125-126.
[11]Gene Edward Veith, Jr., *Loving God with All Your Mind: How to Survive and Prosper as a Christian in the Secular University and Post-Christian Culture* (Westchester, IL: Crossway Books, 1987), pp. 148-149.

brightest minds were sent to the "halls of divinity" of the great universities to study for the ministry. Then it was considered a great privilege to be a "minister of the gospel of Jesus Christ." Even early into this century it was not uncommon to find a "common preacher" who was a Phi Beta Kappa university graduate with at least a graduate degree. Today, most unfortunately, that "honor" has passed to medical doctors and scientists at the expense of the church and (I believe) of the world in which we live.

Yet, "education" in itself is not the total answer, but *understanding, commitment* and *piety* are! What education is supposed to "do" is to make one realize that he or she is *not* an expert on everything; in fact, probably not an expert on much of anything. Most people who have real "bonafide" doctoral degrees realize the degree constitutes relatively little more than a serious "learner's permit!" But thanks in part to Modernism, we have given up the battleground.

The Real Answer: The Priesthood of All Believers

So what is the answer? If many of even the most famous preachers today are ill prepared in terms of knowledge of the Word, where does the "average" Christian go if not to the "one-eyed kings?" Fortunately there is an answer that is rather simple to give, but which is certainly not simplistic nor simple to apply. Do they go to "bonafide" Evangelical scholars who have the credentials, have done their "homework," and know the text? Yes, but this is only part of the answer.

The real answer must come in what has long been called the doctrine of "the priesthood of all believers," that every Christian has equal access to God, *and* equal responsibility in sharing this in meaningful ways with others. If we are going to take the priesthood of all believers seriously,[12] and we *must*, then each individual Christian still has the responsibility to know not only what they believe, but why they believe it, to engage in serious study of the Word and of the world. There is no more biblical idea than the "priesthood of all believers,"

---

[12]Terry L. Miethe, *The New Christian's Guide to Following Jesus* (Minneapolis: Bethany House Publishers, 1984), pp. 103-109, 117-121.

that every Christian is a minister of the Gospel of Jesus Christ according to their talents and abilities and willingness to be challenged by the message of the New Testament.

The simple truth is that every person who claims to be a Christian has a *personal* responsibility to spend the rest of their lives as *serious students* of the text of Scripture! After all, the only way you can be really sure that even the "two-eyed kings" are telling you the truth, giving you the correct information, is if you pay the price to have the background, knowledge, and experience to check it out for yourself. This will mean great personal study, getting a "second opinion" (checking other scholars and "authorities" down through church history), and the willingness to constantly reexamine — or restudy — the data!

In my book *The New Christian's Guide to Following Jesus*, I suggest that new Christians should "develop good 'spiritual' habits," i.e.:

> (1) Begin and end every day with prayer. Prayer is basically conversation with God. Remember: you can talk to God anytime you want! (2) Read and meditate on a Bible passage daily — usually no more than a paragraph. I suggest in the beginning from the New Testament. (3) Never miss Church worship unless absolutely necessary! (4) Set aside a time each day for solitude; i.e. private prayer or meditation. (5) Try in some way, by example or word, to share your faith in Christ Jesus daily.[13]

These are good starting points. But if you are ever to get to the place where you do not have to rely on the "one-eyed kings," *you* must take responsibility for your "spiritual" and intellectual life. These two can never really be separated! You must go far beyond the five simple suggestions listed above.

You must pay the high price of serious study in and of the Christian life and in the text of the Bible! "Only *you* can prevent forest fires!" (Another rather familiar saying that rings true.) The point was that each of us as an individual must take responsibility for our own actions. Only *you* can free yourself from dependence on "experts" (one-eyed kings) who are really not adequately prepared to lead you in growing in

---

[13]*Ibid.*, p. 19.

Christ! I guess the reverse would also be true, i.e., "Only *you* can start forest fires." In this case, *you* must start a "fire" in your mind. As the Romans also said: *soli Deo gloria!* (glory to God alone). If *we* would only learn this!

12 The Disciplined Christian

Try always so to live that you will never be part of the problem, but always part of the solution! There are great hordes of Christians out there who are part of the problem, or who will not admit the problem exists, or who are content with complaining about the problem, but we must settle for nothing less than being a real part of the solution.
—*Reflections,* Vol. IV

At this point, the Christian's need to know is abundantly evident. Knowledge, both of the Word (the text of Scripture) and the world (the context in which we live), is essential (1) to *faith itself* (that initial acceptance of Jesus as Lord and Savior). The Bible is clear that we must hear the Word (John 5:24, Rev. 3:20) and we must act upon what we hear (Matt. 7:24, James 1:22). And, how can we respond to what we hear if we do not understand, from our experience in the world, our need for Christ? Even that initial trusting aspect of faith — what John Stott called "a reasoning trust" — must be based on knowledge of our need and who Jesus is.[1]

(2) Knowledge is essential to *faithfulness* (the actual living out of the commitment).[2] Again, we must be "doers of the word, and not merely hearers who delude themselves. For if any one is a hearer of the word and not a doer, he is like a man who looks at his natural face in the mirror . . . and goes away and forgets what kind of person he is" (James 1:22-24). "Forgetting" is a mental act (or lack of it). For us humans, whether we would like to admit it or not, it is sometimes quite intentional. How can we live out what we do not know? How

---

[1] See chapter one, "What Is Faith, Really?," specifically the section on "Trust and Its Basis."
[2] See chapter two, "Isn't it Enough to Just Believe?" and three, "Free in Christ to Know."

can we be faithful to something — or in this case someone, Jesus — if we do not know to what or to whom we are supposed to be faithful? This is why lifelong Bible study is essential for the Christian.

(3) Knowledge is essential to *evangelism* (putting forth an effective witness of the love of God through His Son, Jesus).[3] Evangelism must be based on the example of Jesus and the New Testament. Jesus loved people so much he cried for them (Luke 19:41, John 11:35). It must be intelligent, based on knowledge of the Scripture and of the individuals to whom we are witnessing if it is to be effective. And perhaps most of all, evangelism must be "relational," that is we must be "real" ourselves before we can both show and tell any other person the real Lord.

(4) Knowledge is essential *even to love* (love presupposes knowledge, emotion itself is seated in the mind).[4] If we have learned anything from fundamentalists, it is that just "beating people over the head with the Bible" is not going to accomplish much. "Love is the greatest of all virtues, the characteristic virtue of the Christian faith." If God had not loved us, He would not have sent His Son to save us from our sins. If Jesus had not loved us, He would not have willingly died on the cross for us. When we love someone we love him or her with our minds. "'Agape' is not merely an emotional experience, it is a deliberate principle of the mind."[5]

(5) And certainly, knowledge is essential to *Christian living* (service to God and to man).[6] The "faithfulness" we mentioned in number two above cannot be accomplished without lives lived in service to both God and man — though some people seem to think they can be "faithful" without doing anything much for God or for fellow human beings. As a minister, I have met many church members who seem to think — by their actions, or lack thereof — that they can be "faithful" (live out their commitment to God) simply by saying that they

---

[3]See chapter five, "Building the Faith in Our World;" and six, "Free to Win Souls to Christ."
[4]See chapter seven, "Free to Love the Unlovely."
[5]See p. 83.
[6]See chapter nine, "Renewing the Mind: Key to Christian Living."

are committed (and never going to church) or by simply filling a pew. It is certainly true that there is a great difference between that initial act we call "salvation" and the lifelong process known as "sanctification," but it is equally true that the New Testament is clear that one assumes the other. And, knowledge is necessary for any kind of effective "service." It is also clear that Christians are called not just to give, but to give sacrificially — of their time, talents, and material possessions — in the New Testament.[7]

We must remember why this need to know is so very important, what in fact we are really seeking. Further, we need to say a word or two about how this need to know translates into practical reality.

Seek First The Kingdom of God

Always remember to "seek first His kingdom and His righteousness; and all these things shall be added unto you" (Matt. 6:33). The primary reason Christians need to seek knowledge is to concentrate on striving to perfect our relationship to God, our heavenly Father. "Seek" carries the meaning of earnestly, intensely searching for, living for, a thing. Jesus emphasized the importance of this seeking by adding the word "first." This should be our top priority — above *all* others.

I was impressed with the attitude — the correct attitude — a former student of mine from Australia expressed in a letter to me sometime back. He said:

> I decided some time ago that what I had to concentrate on was being a faithful Christian. *I also decided that being faithful had more to do with my relationship to God and my relationships with my brothers and sisters in Christ than it did with the fulfillment of my particular career goals. (The favors I was going to do for God)* [emphasis added]. However, I am also very committed to the cause of Christians living out their Christianity in a meaningful and loving manner within the world of academia. And in particular within the philosophical community. So I'm going to

---

[7]See chapter 16, "Christian Stewardship" in Miethe, *The New Christian's Guide to Following Jesus*, pp. 97-101.

give it all I've got and go as far as God allows — or until it seems that I can more meaningfully express my faith in another context.

It was a genuine God-given privilege to have taught — and to have been taught by — a student like that. He understands that the primary importance of knowledge is in seeking first to know Him, then to serve Him. In his case, this student wants to do this in the world of academics, and in particular within the philosophical community if God allows, but what is most important — and the student knows this — is to be living out precisely that attitude in any community of which you are a part. Douglas Gresham, in his excellent book *Lenten Lands*, quotes his stepfather C. S. Lewis as having said: "It is not important to succeed, but to do right. The rest is up to God."[8] Amen.

It is *not* wrong to be genuinely concerned about these "other things" (the things of the world, that is, food, clothing; or, even academics). But it is terribly wrong to put them first. We must not do this. Jesus had already said, in what we call the "Lord's Prayer" (Matt. 6:9-13), that we need to start with coming to God and His kingdom and His will.

D. Martyn Lloyd-Jones says:

> Of course you are interested in life and in the world; but you do not start by saying, "Give us this day our daily bread." You start like this: "Our Father which art in heaven, hallowed be thy name. Thy kingdom come. Thy will be done on earth, as it is in heaven." And then and only then, "Give us this day our daily bread." "Seek ye first" — not "your daily bread," but "the kingdom of God and his righteousness."[9]

What Jesus is saying here is that our mind, our heart, and our desire must be set *first* on God, His kingdom, His righteousness. This should take absolute priority! "He is not telling His hearers how to make themselves Christians; but He is telling them how to behave because they are Christian." Once

---

[8]Douglas H. Gresham, *Lenten Lands: My Childhood with Joy Davidman and C.S. Lewis* (New York: Macmillan, 1988), p. 129.

[9]D. Martyn Lloyd-Jones, *Studies in the Sermon on the Mount*, Vol. 2 (Grand Rapids, MI: Wm. B. Eerdmans, 1970), p. 143.

we become a Christian the process is not finished. Growing in Christ involves a constant desire to know God more and more; to conform to His standards, to His holiness; to get to the place where we are feeding on the meat, as Paul says, not just on milk (Heb. 5:12-14).

In Hebrews 6:1-2 Paul actually tells us to leave "the elementary teaching about Christ" and to "press on to maturity, not laying again a foundation of repentance from dead works and of faith toward God . . . ." But how can we progress on to maturity if we have not studied diligently His Word, do not know what it says, why it says it, and how to apply the Bible to our daily lives? It is only by feeding on the "meat" of the Word that we can make progress toward maturity. This is each Christian's responsibility and privilege.

Paul tells us in Ephesians 4:13-14 that we must strive to attain to "the knowledge of the Son of God, to a mature man, to the measure of the stature which belongs to the fullness of Christ." And that by so doing "we are no longer to be children, tossed here and there by waves and carried about by every wind of doctrine, by the trickery of men, by craftiness in deceitful scheming . . . ." Yes, the Christian's need to know the Word and the world is absolutely crucial for maturing in Christ.

We are not only to seek His kingdom, but His righteousness. I know many Christians who are actively seeking His kingdom, but not His righteousness. I was once one of them. Yet, the two must be sought together. We cannot really seek His kingdom, His standards, applied in our lives as individuals or in our society until we also seek His righteousness, His holiness. "Blessed are those who hunger and thirst for righteousness, for they shall be satisfied" (Matt. 5:6). Again, Lloyd-Jones says it well:

> Yes, this is it. The Christian is seeking righteousness, seeking to be like Christ, seeking positive holiness and to be more and more holy, growing in grace and in the knowledge of the Lord. This is the way to increase your faith.[10]

---

[10]*Ibid.*, p. 144.

The truth of the matter is this: Christianity is as true or as valid as a mathematical formula. But Christianity differs from these formulas in that its truth always has personal, moral implications and applications. His kingdom becomes an earthly validity only as we strive to live out His moral standards in our lives. Growing in *knowledge* is essential to growing in holiness.

Diligence Is Vital

Christians must understand that seeking after God's kingdom and righteousness is a *lifelong process.* This growing in faith can only translate into practical reality with the realization that *diligence* is an essential part of this process. Hebrews 11:6 tells us, "He that cometh to God must believe that he is and that he is a rewarder of them that diligently seek him" (KJV). Christians who do not understand the importance of diligence to the process of maturing in the faith miss many of the blessings in this life.

Diligence is defined as "constant, careful effort; perseverance." It is not nearly so important where we are on the road, as it is that we are on it, moving toward maturity. God will do His part, you can be sure of that, but we must do ours. Too many people have a "fun and games" approach to the Christian faith and to the church. As a minister, I can tell you from much experience that many want a rich spiritual reward without the essential investment of a disciplined effort in Bible study, worship, giving, and fellowship. Christians who spend only one or two hours a week in Bible study are not very serious about their faith.

Yes, there is something very practical that you can do to grow in Christ: spend more *time* in prayer, reading and studying your Bible, reading Christian literature. Go to the minister of your church and ask for good Christian material that you can start studying. Go to a Christian bookstore and get to know the manager so that you can become aware of the best and newest material. We must fill our minds with that which will build up, edify — to His honor and glory, not to our own. Yet, *no one* can do it for us: pope, priest, or pastor! We must discipline our lives if we are to grow. Sometimes I just want to cry out from the depths of my soul with an excruciatingly painful scream: "Oh, for a moral man who does not claim to be a Christian." I know there are such. Or: "Oh, for a Christian who knows that he is not a moral man." A Christian who doesn't have to play at the game of "righteous indignation" where the only real rule is judging others. A Christian who isn't a classic bigot, who gives another the benefit of the doubt, and who realizes that he is not in the business of judging another because of his own sin. Often I feel like the "harlots of old" (for example Rahab) had more integrity — and humility — than modern day yuppie/establishment Christians. The comfortable — and I might add, often selfish — lifestyle of the yuppie hardly expresses the message of Jesus, the suffering servant.

Gene Edward Veith, Jr. in his book, *Loving God with All Your Mind: How to Survive and Prosper as a Christian In the Secular University and Post-Christian Culture*, says: "Christians with academic gifts need to use them to defend the Christians who do not have them. It is precisely because there is so much error in the world today that there is such a great need for truth."[11] Veith ends his *excellent* book by speaking of a vision he and I most definitely share:

> If we are going through another Dark Age, it may be that learning will again survive, as it always has, in the Christian Church. I have a vision of Christians meeting together to discuss fine points of theology and other ideas when no one else is interested in abstract thinking. I picture the Christian colleges — I have not said enough about them as alternatives to secular academia — as enclaves of the liberal arts while the public colleges have all become sophisticated trade schools. I imagine Christians reading their Bibles and other books, while everyone else is watching television.

Veith dreams — longs for as I do — the day when "Christians, as they have in the past, will help usher in a new Renaissance,

---

[11]Gene Edward Veith, Jr., *Loving God with All Your Mind: How to Survive and Prosper as a Christian In the Secular University and Post-Christian Culture* (Westchester, IL: Crossway Books, 1987), p. 148. Just before the part I quote from Veith, he quotes (p. 147) the passage from C. S. Lewis which is part of the dedication of this book.

a flowering of the arts and sciences, a renewal of Western Culture, and a revival of Biblical spirituality."[12]

If this book has done nothing else for you, it is my hope that you have a better appreciation for why it is so important for you as a Christian to know in *Whom* you believe, *what* you believe, *why* you believe it, and *how* you can apply it to Christian living and witnessing. Too many Christians are playing the game of success by the standards of the world. Remember, Christian, Jesus called us to be faithful, faithful to Him, not to be successful either in the eyes of the world *or* of other Christians. Always remember to "seek first His kingdom and His righteousness!" And this is my prayer, "Dear Lord, for each and every Christian, help him or her to desire your knowledge, wisdom, love and diligence, as they seek to grow in faith (understanding and commitment) and service." Amen (so be it)!

Postscript: A Word of Warning

I should say a word here by way of a "warning." What I am about to say is too important for an "endnote." In fact, I have never known anything more deserving of a "P.S." Knowledge *is* dangerous! Even knowledge of the truth. For with knowledge comes responsibility, and with responsibility a "burning" desire to *be* even more of what you are already becoming; and then, to do something about what you are becoming.

The Bible tells us that one of the important reasons for the Old Testament Law was to teach us about right and wrong, to make us aware of sin. In the New Testament we learn that Jesus paid the price for our sins and that we, with His strength and knowledge of His Word and the world, can live for Him, that we have the glorious privilege and serious responsibility of *becoming* like Him and of acting on His Word!

Very recently, I received a letter from a friend. This friend and I originally became acquainted when he phoned to ask me a question during an hour-long radio talk show program on which I was the guest. Later he wrote me a very gracious

---

[12]*Ibid.*, p. 149.

letter of support and this started a year of correspondence during which he has been introduced to many of my favorite Christian authors; among them C.S. Lewis. Now he writes me saying:

> I really do need to make some changes [in my life.] I feel very restless these days for a variety of reasons. I am a "task oriented" person who needs to feel that I am accomplishing something of value. My business just "does not do it." I often feel like the writer of Ecclesiastes when he said that "all is vanity!" [Join the club!] I am considering going back to school but do not know if I have either the dedication or power of concentration [he does] to do that. But I *am* going to make a change of some sort since I am no longer that "contented person who wrote a letter of support to a very special [I have tried to dissuade him regarding this many times] man."

We have joked many times about his "umbrella" [understanding of Christianity] becoming much bigger these days.

I wrote him back and said:

> Feeling *"very restless"* [emphasis added] is the price one pays for knowing Truth (reality) and "responsibility" and in general for having knowledge and a "holy" umbrella! I have been paying it for over twenty-five years. Remember there are no easy answers or necessarily easy solutions and "knowledge" exacts a "terrible" price. I should have warned you about the price of knowledge, and faith!

This whole book, in a real way, has been about the "price" *for* or *of* faith. "Easy believeism" is as foreign to biblical Christianity as is the East to the West. Even salvation which is free was not — and is not — without great cost. This last sentence may seem like a contradiction, but it is not! Yes, my friends, "ignorance is bliss" to a large degree. But, I believe the "rewards" of striving to know God in a fuller way are well worth the "price" that comes with truth and responsibility.

Yet, there will be some very definite implications to *your life* in your search for knowledge, for truth — for *God*. All this is not "easy" and you should be very leery of anyone who tells you that it is easy. In my own life, it seems that almost every time I have just made a renewed commitment very seriously, or have been making real progress, that is when Satan attacks. And as strange as it may seem, Satan can even use Christians (sometimes people who claim to be your best friends, not unlike Job's of old) to mount the attack against you.

When Satan has battered and all but beaten you, and he thinks you are close to "throwing in the towel," he doesn't let up! He continually brings up old things, and anything he can, to try to push you over the edge, to totally defeat you. As contradictory as this may sound, it is when you are at your *weakest* that you must be *strongest!* In such times, which try the very depths of one's soul, you must especially turn to God for *His* strength and power. "Even so great men great losses should endure," (Shakespeare, *Julius Caesar*, Act IV, Scene III). But I say: Truly great men great losses *must* endure, but not one minute more than is absolutely necessary! Great men, as they endure great suffering, are reaching down into the depths of their being, marshaling greater energy even as they reach down, to rise again victorious!

Ye have been warned! But remember the rest of the story: "*It takes 'willpower' to make a dream come true!*" But what is "willpower"? Only man, as a rational animal, possesses will. The Latin "volition" means "to will." Will is the ability of human self-determination. The "will" of a human is the strongest possible assent to, rational determination to do a thing, to accomplish no matter what. It is more than just intellect or appetite. In scholastic thought will always ultimately aims at a good. Goodness is one of the original ("transcendental") aspects of being.

While the human will is essentially free, it is often restricted in the exercise of its freedom by imagination (or more properly the lack of it), emotion, habit. So what is "willpower?" And, why is it necessary to make a dream come true? "Willpower" is the unique human ability to rally all one's mental, spiritual, and physical energy to do, to achieve (really what the Greeks called "agony") — to never give up. It makes dreams come true because dreams can only "live" when brought to actualization by the power of the will!

In Christ we can truly be "Overcomers" — a very special people, not necessarily better than the rest, but who stand apart nevertheless. They take every agony life throws them and "by rite of passage" rise again victorious, stronger than ever before. Knowing that more times of trial will come, they will meet them (even though the pain will be greater each time and therefore will be always more difficult) with greater strength gained "by rite of passage." This is what makes them Overcomers.

Or, were these "Overcomers" destined to be so? Only God knows and we can never take for granted that we are "Overcomers," but there is, I believe, such a class of people who thus stand apart from the common man, who are rooted in the ordinary but who are called to be extraordinary.

Now, go and seek and experience the wonders of being created in the image of our great God!

Appendices

A A View of Faith and Learning

Here I go again playing devil's advocate, or being the lightning-rod to rekindle a critical discussion of a most important subject. I hope some contemporary "Calvin" does not decide I am a present-day Michael Servetus (1511-1553) and try to help me meet my Maker in the same way Servetus did in Geneva! I am not going to be so stupid as to tell the "uninformed" how Servetus met his end for fear that some copycat might try to renew a very old tradition.

In the 1960s, a term that was used quite often in regard to the idea of integrating an individual's personal faith and a liberal arts education in Christian colleges was "a view of faith and learning."[1] The "traditional" or "classical" view was that all truth was indeed God's truth, but all truth had to be integrated in view of a type of "hierarchy" with biblical truth at the top, i.e., "we take captive every thought to make it obedient to Christ" (2 Cor. 10:3-5). Truth in a different academic discipline, say anthropology, had to be interpreted in light of what the Bible says and reconciled with biblical teaching. This, it was said, was integration, taking every thought to Christ.

The First View

In this view, Theology was the queen of the sciences. But there are limits to this view, for example: (1) The biblical data has to be interpreted correctly; that is, according to the best

---

[1]This section is the result, in part, of discussions with my good friend, Robert W. Yarbrough, Ph.D., University of Aberdeen, Scotland; formerly Assistant Professor of New Testament and Theology at Wheaton College (Illinois); and now, Associate Professor of New Testament Studies at Covenant Theological Seminary in St. Louis.

exegesis, in context, etc. (2) The truth from psychology — just to choose a discipline at random — must be allowed to make a difference. Said psychological truth (for example) may help us to see what the Bible has in fact been saying all along. (3) The plain fact of the matter is that the Bible (though we might wish that it did) *does not speak on every issue in every discipline.* Free will, logical extrapolation, and "common sense" are not only permitted, but required. Either view can be pushed to unacceptable extremes, i.e., the *first* to a biblical legalism that interprets all truth in light of one's own theological presuppositions and prejudice; or the *second* view to a biblical liberalism that interprets all truth as being totally equal and therefore relative to each other.

The Second View

The second view of integration, and the current view at *many* Christian colleges is that *all truth exists on an equal par, or level.* Because this is (assumed to be) true, biblical truth has to give way to truth in other areas, say for example in psychology or sociology. Instead of the Bible, and specifically the Old Testament, being the foundation of an understanding of the nature of man, "truth" in anthropology informs us equally about the nature of man and his relationships. This has two rather *devastating* results: (1) Instead of trying to understand all of God's truth *as God's truth* and therefore the truth (in psychology) must be consistent with what Scripture teaches, often it is assumed that Scripture *must* be modified in light of the "truth" in other areas. Theological truth must be modified by the truth found in anthropology. (2) Because all truth is God's truth, the "subtle" implication is that anyone trained in any discipline is just as able to interpret ("expert" in interpreting) biblical truth as is anyone else.

Real Integration

If one holds this second option, integration is viewed in a much different way. This new view has a theoretical (in terms of methodology, as we have just seen) implication and a very important (and dangerous) practical application. Many

Christian scholars, who teach at Christian colleges, have a "Sunday School" level of knowledge[2] in theology or biblical studies and a Ph.D. in another area, say political science, from a secular school, say Cornell. This Ph.D. thinks that he/she is an expert in theology and can pontificate on theology and on integration. Such a scholar, trained in a "secular" discipline at a "secular" university, thinks he/she knows a lot about theology and actually only has a Ph.D. in another totally unrelated discipline. Very often he/she has *no* formal training in theology *or* biblical studies *or* biblical languages. Often such a person is also proud that his/her "secular" university training did not "taint" him/her or affect *his/her* faith. How naive! Because of a lack of understanding of his/her own presuppositions (and of integration), of the purpose of and influence of education in a certain discipline, and a lack of formal training in biblical knowledge, Jesus may just turn out — to him (and even more unfortunately, to his/her students) — to be the first radical "right wing" political conservative, i.e.: "Heaven is only for right wing Republicans!"

Further, this scholar thinks just because he happens to be Christian and has "Christian experience" that he is an expert in theology and what the Scripture teaches. This is *incredibly dangerous* because it fools that scholar (1) into thinking he is doing integration and (2) fools his students into thinking they are getting integration when his/her professor really has no formal knowledge of theology or biblical truth, and does not even understand the methodology of integration. Biblical Truth is fundamental and foundational to all truth!

Yet, all truth is God's truth. The "truth" as seen — discovered — in other academic disciplines must be allowed to be a factor in our world view. But the "truth" of these other academic disciplines must be judged — when it truly comes into

---

[2] By this I mean no formal training in regard to the biblical data. It is quite wrong to assume that just because one has a Ph.D. level of knowledge in — by way of example only — psychology or anthropology that this scholar has an equal level of knowledge in regard to the biblical data. It is true, many of the skills one learns in achieving a Ph.D. in any discipline can be used profitably to study the formal content of another area, *but the formal content of that area must still be formally studied.*

conflict with Scripture — by the best exegesis of the biblical text. If, and this can be a big "if", the Scripture really contradicts the "truth" of the "secular" academic discipline, then another answer or other answers must be *seriously* explored within the academic discipline until the supposed conflict or contradiction is resolved.

Two insights are helpful here: (1) There are genuine antinomies (that is a contradiction between two principles each taken to be true, or between inferences correctly drawn from such principles). At least, there are serious conflicts between principles which need to be acknowledged. And (2) often, what "appears" as a serious contradiction is only the appearance of contradiction. Logically one affirmation is truly only a contradiction of another when the one is asserting the direct opposite of the other at the same time, in the same way (or context).

In a Christian college or university, all truth must be interpreted in light of what the Bible says and reconciled with biblical teaching. Further, biblical Truth must be understood formally, i.e., examined by the proper scholarly methods of the disciplines involved, e.g., theology, biblical languages, biblical studies!

B The Christian and Debate

Many Christians do not think debate is important *or* valid. "Why waste your time debating," because: (1) "Debating never changes any one's mind, let alone that of the debater." Or, (2) "Debating is sacrilegious because as Christians *we* know the truth and should never question, only accept what we already know." Both positions, as we will see, are seriously flawed.

"Debating" and "Arguing" are Not the Same

It is important to point out that "debating" and "arguing" are not the same! As a freshman at a major state university, I quickly learned there were three subjects you should not argue because you could never win. Everyone agreed — at least tacitly — that they were of such a nature and there was evidence for many differing opinions, as to almost preclude the possibility of any kind of real agreement. In the mid sixties, as now, behind this statement was the assumption that truth was relative. The subjects were: politics, sex, and religion. Yet, in our free time about all we did was to argue — yes — politics, sex, and religion. A poignant Latin phrase comes to mind: *de asini umbra disceptare*. Disraeli, in his novel *Sybil*, freely rendered the Latin as "little things affect little minds." How true. Perhaps Disraeli was more "refined" than either we were (as university freshmen) or the Romans.

Certainly there is some truth to the idea that "arguing" can be, and is often a meaningless waste of time. The Latin language, it seems, has an excellent saying for almost every occasion. The Latin saying, *disputandi pruritus ecclesiarum scabies* is translated: "The theologian's urge to debate is an incurable disease." Sir Henry Wotton (1568-1639), an English poet and diplomat, wrote this sentence, literally "an itch for disputation is the mange of the churches," in his *A Panegyric to King Charles*. Yet by the time I was a senior in Bible college, I had learned that arguing — sometimes most of the night — just to argue with someone who disagreed with you and who just wanted to argue for the sake of argument was indeed a waste of precious time.

The Grand Tradition of Debate

Well, if debate and argument are not the same, what is the difference? To answer this question we need to look at "debate" as it is now practiced and as it was practiced in the eighteenth and early nineteenth centuries. Of course, everyone recognizes that the "staged confrontations" we witness in the name of "presidential debates" are not debates at all! They are, at best, forums where the two candidates get half of the allotted time to state their positions in a pabulum form that would starve a baby!

Today, in our colleges and universities, debate as it is practiced has more to do with *style* than content. Student debaters are taught to "make points," to destroy, make fun of the opponent, to use any tactic that will help you *win*. If, along the way, you happen to have the better information, facts, "truth" to support your "performance" then fine, but *do* everything — use any tactic — you can to win! If this is what "debate" is all about, then I agree that "debating never changes any one's mind, let alone that of the debater." "Debate" practiced thus is really not meant to "change any one's mind," but only appear to win an argument.

But the eighteenth and early nineteenth centuries had a great tradition of real "debate". "Debate" was an honored method for "getting all the facts on the table," for pursuing the breath and depth of a subject in an attempt to discern the *truth of a matter!* Proponent and opponent alike were interested, not in making points, but honestly presenting the very best evidence for what they believed to be true. Such debates were important events in shaping thought, the course of discussion in the future, and eventually public opinion on a subject. These debates could go on for hours and involve several days. They were often then printed in a book which also advanced the pursuit of truth.[1] This view of debate can be as important today as it was then, if practiced with intelligence and integrity!

When Christians Debate

If as a Christian, you are going to engage in debate permit me to give you some important advice regarding "method." *First,* (and one of the two *most* important aspects) *do your homework*: prepare, prepare, prepare and prepare. There *must* be no exception to this rule! When I was debating a very famous Roman Catholic Archbishop, I went with a well prepared manuscript intending to "shed more light than heat" on the subject and to answer important questions regarding the topic that had either not been raised before or answered adequately. This debate was to be repeated twice in two days to different audiences. The second day it was taped for public T.V. On the second day, my "opponent" the Archbishop started by apologizing to our audience for his erroneous preconceived opinions about me and said he was going to abbreviate his remarks so "Dr. Miethe would have more time to speak." What a compliment.

Second, as best you can, *know your audience.* This is not as hard as you might expect. You should at least have a good idea by the nature of the occasion, where you are asked to debate, and by whom — in general — what type of audience you will be addressing. If you misjudge this some, it will not be a serious matter *if you have prepared very well* because you can modify your presentation according to the needs of the situation. Do you want to speak to your supporters in the audience, your opponent, or those people in the audience who are against your position? My contention is that you should try to speak to all three. "How" you present your message (articulation and personality) is as important as "what" you say.

Third, ask yourself *what it is you want to accomplish* in the

---

[1] See Alexander Campbell's published debates for examples. There were published debates with Rev. N. L. Rice, Rev. W. L. MacCalla, John Walker, Robert Owen, and Rt. Rev. John B. Purcell. See also the two debates with Tony Flew listed in "Other works by Terry L. Miethe."

debate. Do you want to show clearly the differences in the two positions (assuming there are only two and, as a Christian, you should have the integrity to admit the true situation in this regard) or build on the commonalties? Actually, in reality this can be a false dilemma. As Christians, we should always try to do both, for an accurate statement of the evidence will show both are usually true, at least in part. Yet, of course, you will focus on the major facts of the case you are presenting.

Fourth, and equal with preparation, *be gracious*, Christian! I have known several famous Christian debaters who won the "argument," but lost the "debate"! — They had the best content *and* the worst personality. Consequently, the audience went away with more emotional sympathy for the atheist opponent, and therefore for his position! We *can* often build bridges even as we clarify differences.

True, you most probably will not "win" over your opponents in the audience or your actual opponent just because of one debate. But you can give your supporters in the audience, who may know some of the opponents, material so they can continue the debate in the gracious manner with which you began it. You may also be able to make a "friend" out of your opponent for the future which may be of inestimable value!

Once, while I was driving around my good friend (and world famous atheist philosopher) Antony G. N. Flew, he said to me: "Terry, why should I believe a man when he speaks to me about heavenly things, if I cannot believe him when he speaks to me about earthly things?" Christians, above all others, must have integrity when they speak about, or *do*, anything! I have been involved in debating Tony Flew twice and we have built a friendship which I value highly.[2] Tony is one of the finest, most ethical men I have ever met! He is simply wrong, I believe, in holding that God does not exist. I hope and pray that my friendship will be used to honor and glorify my Lord in Tony's life!

---

[2]See Terry L. Miethe (ed.), *Did Jesus Rise from the Dead? The Resurrection Debate* with Gary R. Habermas and Antony G. N. Flew (San Francisco: Harper & Row, 1987); and Terry L. Miethe and Antony G. N. Flew, *Does God Exist? A Believer and an Atheist Debate* (San Francisco: Harper Collins, 1991).

Christians should be involved in debate because we have a scriptural mandate to be out there in the market place (Acts 17:17-34), to serve as salt, light, and leaven (Matt. 5:13-16, 13:33), to give an answer for the hope that is in us (1 Peter 3:15), to set forth our case (Isa. 41:21). (This is the answer to the second reason in the first paragraph regarding why we should not debate.) And, we must debate with great preparation, intellectual honesty, personal integrity, and simple graciousness. It should never be that the atheist is found to be *more of any of these* than his Christian opponent!

C The Limits of Science

If you will permit me a "small" tautology (after all, the world allowed Darwin a tautology — in the form of his theory of the survival of the fittest — for over one hundred years), I will say that the place to begin this chapter is in the beginning. The beginning involves two disclaimers: (1) I am not, by way of academic training, a *scientist,* nor am I (2) strictly speaking a *philosopher of science.* The second is true because certainly neither of my two Ph.D.'s are in philosophy of science. At most American universities to be admitted into a Ph.D. program in philosophy of science one has to hold at least a bachelor's degree in a field of science. Thus in the sense of formal academic training, I am neither a "scientist" nor a "philosopher of science." (It would be helpful if others would make such appropriate disclaimers *in print* before they started "pontificating" on a subject.)

Yet, I want to discuss: "The Limits of Science." Now perhaps my two disclaimers are *not* so condemning that you should close this book, arise from your seats and go out to play ball or something. For the issues I am about to address are *very* important to the "average" Christian and the issues also are not strictly speaking, in the modern sense, "science" nor have they ever been.

It also needs to be clear from the beginning that I am not condemning science nor am I throwing out the proverbial baby with the bath water. In this case the "baby" is science and the "bath water" is the incorrect thinking and faulty conclusions of some scientists. There is much that could be said, and needs to be said, in a chapter like this which I will not have time to say. For instance, one could outline the development of modern science (what I call "the new science" — what others call "the modern mind") by analyzing the historical development of the revolution in Western thought and educational assumptions of the modern world from the Graeco-Roman or Classical *weltanschauung* that flourished until the fourth century AD through the triumph of the Christian world view which dominated Western civilization until the seventeenth century when the rise of modern science inaugurated a third way — "The Modern Mind."

One could introduce evolution in terms of a historical perspective on the evolution of evolutionary ideas. A scholar's task, indeed any educated person's is to "contribute [more] light than heat to a discussion."[1] I hope within the limitations of this chapter to accomplish that. I hope to make some clear statements of the real issues at hand in the seemingly never-ending debate between science and religion. To this end, I introduce the following sections: "The Nature and Definition of Science"; "Three Scientific World Views in History"; "The Case of Darwinism"; and "Some Clear Statements About the Issues."

The Nature and Definition of Science

In large part, what is at issue here is the very definition of "science." "The modern mind," or as I call it "the new science" defines what constitutes "science" in terms of a very restrictive methodology. "Science" is synonymous with the method of observing repeatable phenomena in a laboratory. Thus according to the Oxford Dictionary, "Science" must involve proof and certainty, must not depart from what can be generated rigorously from immediate observation, and must not speculate beyond presently observable processes. That is a woefully inadequate construal of science, and does indeed stick one with a methodic — if not a positively positivist — conception.

In the history of the Western world, science was defined as the search for truth about reality, all reality! This included not only the physical, but the metaphysical. It is also undeniably true that, historically, modern science as we know it was born

---

[1] See Woodrow Wilson's *The Spirit of Learning* quoted in part in the *Phi Beta Kappa Handbook for New Members*, p. 4.

THE LIMITS OF SCIENCE

out of a Christian Metaphysic or world view. C. S. Lewis, talking about the Uniformity of Nature (our belief that nature acts and will always act in the same way which is the basis for all science), says:

> This faith — the preference (in the Uniformity of Nature) — is it a thing we can trust? Or is it only the way our minds happen to work? ... The answer depends on the Metaphysic one holds. If all that exists is Nature, the great mindless interlocking event ... then clearly there is not the slightest ground for supposing that our sense of fitness and our consequent faith in uniformity tell us anything about a reality external to ourselves. ... It can be trusted only if quite a different Metaphysic is true. If the deepest thing in reality, the Fact which is the source of all other facthood, is a thing in some degree like ourselves — if it is a Rational Spirit and we derive our rational spirituality from It — then indeed our conviction can be trusted.

Lewis goes on to say:

> The sciences logically require a metaphysic of this sort. Our greatest natural philosopher thinks it is also the metaphysic out of which they originally grew. Professor Whitehead points out that centuries of belief in a God who combined "the personal energy of Jehovah" with "the rationality of a Greek philosopher" first produced that firm expectation of systematic order which rendered possible the birth of modern science. Men became scientific because they expected Law in Nature because they believed in a Legislator. In most modern scientists this belief has died: it will be interesting to see how long their confidence in uniformity survives it.[2]

It is interesting to see the actual context of the quote that Lewis takes from Whitehead. In *Science and the Modern World*, Whitehead says:

> But for science something more is wanted than a general sense of the order in things. ... I do not think, however, that I have even yet brought out the *greatest contribution of medievalism to the formation of the scientific movement* [emphasis added].

---

[2]C. S. Lewis, *Miracles: A Preliminary Study* (New York: Macmillian, 1947), pp. 108-109.

How has this conviction been so vividly implanted on the European mind?

When we compare this tone of thought in Europe with the attitude of other civilisations when left to themselves, there seems but one source for its origin. It must come from the medieval insistence on the rationality of God, conceived as with the personal energy of Jehovah and with the rationality of a Greek philosopher. Every detail was supervised and ordered: the search into nature could only result in the vindication of the faith in rationality. Remember that I am not talking of the explicit belief of a few individuals. What I mean is the impress on the European mind arising from the unquestioned faith of centuries.... My only point is to understand how it arose. My explanation is that the faith in the possibility of science, generated antecedently to the development of modern scientific theory, is an unconscious derivative from medieval theology.[3]

It is really when one defines the goal of science to be the discovery of explanatory truths (not truth as it ought to be stated; by using the nonexistent plural for truth one has already put one's self in a camp which is totally against the historic position of Western thought via even the possibility of a unified field of knowledge) about the *appropriate domain of reality* that we get into trouble. After all, who decides, and by what method, what constitutes "the appropriate domain of reality." Of course, if one accepts the positivistic definition then one is forced to define science to the merely repeatable and observable physical world.

Thus part of the problem is a conception which defines "science" strictly by its methodology. According to this view what constitutes science must be pursued under a variety of methodological constraints. Truth which does not pass the required methodological criteria is not a proper part of science, and therefore, by definition, is not true. Also topics for which the stipulated methodology are inappropriate (e.g., history, psychology, religion, metaphysics, and anything which cannot be duplicated in a laboratory) are not scientific concerns. (Except, of course, when a "scientist" wants to make a

---

[3] Alfred North Whitehead, *Science and the Modern World* (New York: Mentor Books, The New American Library of World Literature, Inc., 1925), pp. 13-14.

pronouncement in one of these above mentioned areas and then he or she is oftentimes considered an expert.) This view of science as defined *only* by its method has fallen into disfavor with many philosophers of science.

Yet, the real problem even here is that some scientists themselves go beyond their own method, making claims to truth that their own methodological constraints do not allow. Creationists would have fewer grounds for quarrel with their opponents if alternatives, say, to flood geology did not make claims about what mechanisms had really accounted for various observables, or what the age of the earth really was, or whether species had really evolved out of ancestor species. In other words, if the method was in fact allowed to remain neutral as a method! (It should be added here that Creationists must also allow the same neutrality of method, if the method is to be defined so narrowly.)

But assume for argument's sake that "the new science" or the empirical laboratory method or "the modern mind" is the only valid method of science. What does this tell us about origins? *Nothing!* Donald M. MacKay, the well-known British scientist, in his *Science and the Quest for Meaning*, asks the question: Can science and technology provide an answer to the quest for meaning?

> My answer, as you can see, is ultimately "no." I don't, on the other hand, think they do anything to destroy the meaning of the mystery of our world when properly understood; and they do, I suggest, enlarge our understanding. . . . On ultimate questions of the meaning of the whole show, however, they are systematically silent, *because these are not scientific questions* [emphasis added]. But — and this is the point — the fact that they are not scientific questions doesn't mean that they are improper questions for the scientist or anyone else to ask as a human being. It means only that if they are to be answered, the answers will have to come from outside the system within which the game of science is defined. It's like chess-playing. If someone says, "Let's play chess," and someone else asks, "Why?" a question has arisen that the rules of chess are not framed to answer.
>
> What I've tried to show, in particular, is that Christian theism is far from being an enemy of science: it actually offers the most rational basis for the practice of science as but one

aspect of the obedience that the creator requires of us and our world. There is no question of having to isolate Christianity from science in order to maintain peace between them. Rather, I suggest, they belong together as naturally as root and fruit: there is in principle an organic unity between biblical Christian faith and natural science.[4]

Once the scientist, so limited by his own method, stops doing repeatable laboratory experiments and recording results and starts talking about what these results mean in the context of the world he has taken off the "hat" of scientist and has in fact put on the "hat" of the "philosopher of science." And once the scientist starts relating these experiments and findings to the question of origins he puts on the "hat" of "philosopher" or "theologian" with metaphysical presuppositions. That is to say that the question of origins, whether one accepts "the new science" or not, cannot strictly be a "scientific" question, but must of necessity be a metaphysical, historical, philosophical and theological question.

I should point out here that some "creation scientists" have perhaps themselves been too quick to accept the very limited methodological constraints of "the new science" or "the modern mind" as the *only* valid methodology of science really for knowing truth. These creationists take their definition of science directly from the aforementioned one in the Oxford Dictionary. This, I believe, has gotten them into all sorts of trouble.[5]

Of course, the question remains: Why insist that one should ignore certain sources of knowledge simply because they do not fall within some conventional boundaries of scientific methodology — especially when (so it is currently argued) those boundaries have been to great extent humanly and historically shaped? Certainly if the real object of science

---

[4]Donald M. MacKay, *Science and the Quest for Meaning* (Grand Rapids, MI: Eerdmans, 1982), pp. 30-31.

[5]It has caused their positions to be tagged as thinly disguised religion (Kitcher and the Overton decision), as dishonest (by most critics) and as scientifically indefensible (by all but a very few critics), because it looks as though they simply have not produced what holding their present position would demand of them.

is to get at the truth then *a priori* limitations based on the method of acquiring information about the nature and history of the world are a bit hard to understand. But I must be clear here: I am not condemning the empirical method as necessary for experimentation in the physical sciences. But I am saying that to say we can *only* have reliable knowledge, and therefore know truth, when a claim can be examined by way of the empirical method, is to rule out of court vast ranges of reality as "unknowable" or as "untrue." *A priori* limitations on science — even by scientists, as we will see in the case of Darwin himself — have often been misguided and counterproductive to real science and its search for truth.

Three Scientific World Views in History

Perhaps the best way to see the fact that the boundaries of science are culturally and historically shaped is to realize there have been at least three grand metaphysical and "scientific" assumptions, that is three world images that have controlled the Western world — the world views of Aristotle, Newton, and Einstein.

Every person has some sort of world image or overall vision of the cosmos which serves as a framework within which specific day-to-day events take place. The primitive with his animistic view and the modern scientist with his mathematical view both conceive of some matrix, and the processes by which events occur within the matrix, in order to explain the phenomena which they observe. The image will be a product of the particular culture of each and will change and develop with the advance of disciplined thinking within that culture. This development can be seen if one compares the cosmological images of Aristotle, Newton, and Einstein which evolved in our European culture.

Aristotle's (384-322 B.C.) world, an image with the Ptolemaic modification of astronomy, was considered "valid" from the time of Aristotle until the time of Galileo Galilei (1564-1642). Sir Isaac Newton's (1642-1727) world image was the outgrowth of the new scientific discipline of the Renaissance and was produced by Newton at the close of the seventeenth century. Albert Einstein's (1879-1955) world image begins about 1915 and is currently being challenged. For instance, the "absolute" of the speed of light has been challenged at the Princeton Institute of Advanced Studies and the Space Research Center and more recently yet by information from space itself. Notice how much drastically shorter is the time period that each scientific world view was considered valid before it was challenged and replaced by a newer scientific world view. Certainly, we can see that scientific knowledge is not final or absolute.

Thus, science is, to some extent, historically and culturally conditioned. Science and world views are continually in flux, as they should be. Let not the church make the mistake it made in the time of the Renaissance:

> Traditional theology had become almost inextricably intertwined with Aristotelian philosophy [and science we might add] and the earth-centred universe. Besides, the earth must be the centre, ran the argument, because it was the scene of Christ's coming. The sun must move because, according to the psalmist, "he rejoices to run his course." ... The story is told that once a certain Father Scheiner mentioned to his superior that he had seen spots on the sun, to which he received the following reply: 'You are mistaken, my son. I have studied Aristotle and he nowhere mentions spots. Try changing your spectacles." (Quoted in A. E. E. McKenzie, *The Major Achievements of Science.* Cambridge University Press.) So great was the authority of ["scientific"] tradition, that it could decide in advance what men might see.[6]

Likewise, we must not make the mistake of assuming that modern science has achieved an absolute definitive understanding of the universe, physical or metaphysical. Therefore allowing it to tell us what could or could not have happened in the distant past or what method is the only valid one by which to discover truth.

The Case of Darwinism

The term "evolution" and its implications has generated

---

[6]T. M. Kitwood, *What is Human?* (Downers Grove: IL: InterVarsity Press, 1970), p. 17.

more hostility, at least among Western Christian thinkers, than any other concept in the modern period. The English noun "evolution" comes from a Latin verb, *evolvere* — to unroll; "*e*" out and "*volvere*", to roll — and signifies the act or process of unfolding or developing. The crucial problems for the Christian can be reduced to three areas: the origin of the universe, the origin of life, and the origin of man and his sociological institutions.

There is no single theory of evolution. There are many theories and they all have the problem of causation as a common factor. Change is undeniable; the question is now and why does it take place? The Christian immediately perceives that the necessity to affirm "absoluteness" (Incarnation, Atonement, Revelation, etc.) concerning the core of the Christian faith, places as great responsibility upon the Christian apologete in our scientific age. Many of the specialized sciences had arisen (as understood by the contemporary mind) relatively recently — Chemistry, Physics, Geology, Psychology, Astronomy, and Biology, etc.[7] These were preliminary for Darwin's work. Evolution as an interpretative principle spread into literature, history, ethics, and religion. No field made any claim to exemption from this principle or orientation. Spencer had produced his system of evolution and it became overt in his *First Principles* before Darwin's *Origin of Species* in 1859.

Evolution as an explanatory principle was proposed by a number of learned men before Charles Darwin, among them Jean Baptiste Lamarck and Erasmus Darwin (Charles' grandfather). Reinhold Treviranus introduced the word *biology* into the nomenclature in his *Biologies oder Philosophies der Lebenden Natur* in 1802. It was Charles Darwin who proposed the machinery of evolution, and claimed that it existed in nature; natural selection, he called it. Thus Darwin's "greatness" was that he provided a causal explanation for genetic change. His idea was accepted very quickly! Once stated it seemed only

---

[7]For good brief chapters on the rise of the sciences besides the larger histories of science see L. L. Woodruff, editor. *The Development of the Sciences* (New Haven, CT: Yale University Press, 1923).

too obvious. Some types are fitter than others. Given the competition, i.e., the struggle for existence, the fitter ones will survive to pass on their traits in their kind. Thus all life (animals, plants, *all life*) will tend to get better and better. This was an inevitable process of nature because Nature itself had evolving machinery built into it.

> That was a little over 100 years ago. By the time of the Darwin Centennial Celebrations at the University of Chicago in 1959, Darwinism was triumphant. At a panel discussion Sir Julian Huxley (grandson to Thomas Henry) affirmed that "the evolution of life is no longer a theory; it is a fact." He added sternly: "we do not intend to get bogged down in semantics and definitions." At about the same time, Sir Gavin de Beer of the British Museum remarked that if a layman sought to "impugn" Darwin's conclusions, it must be the result of "ignorance or effrontery."[8]

Yet, all this time there has been a great debate going on within biology itself about the "facts" of evolutionary theory of which the general public was unaware.

> What was it, then, that Darwin discovered? What was this mechanism of natural selection? Here it comes as a slight shock to learn that Darwin really didn't "discover" anything at all, certainly not in the same way that Kepler, for example, discovered the laws of planetary motion. The *Origin of Species* was not a demonstration but an argument — "one long argument," Darwin himself said at the end of the book — and natural selection was an idea, not a discovery. It was an idea that occurred to him in London in the late 1830's . . .
> While in his country retreat Darwin spent a good deal of time with pigeon fanciers and animal breeders. He even bred pigeons himself. Of particular relevance to him was that breeders bred for certain characteristics (length of feather, length of wool, coloring), and that the offspring of the selected mates often tended to have the desired characteristic more abundantly, or more noticeably, than its parents.[9]

Thus, Darwin got his great idea of Natural selection not really

---

[8]Tom Bethell, "Darwin's Mistake," *Harper's Magazine* (February, 1976), p. 70.
[9]*Ibid.*, p. 72.

from "nature" and certainly not from scientific observation of nature, but from men. If it proved anything — which it did not — it proved that it took intelligent men great effort to make changes. It certainly did not justify making nature into *Nature* and a causal force.

For quite some time Darwin's mechanism was not seriously examined. Finally, T. H. Morgan, renowned geneticist and winner of the Nobel Prize for his work in mapping the chromosomes of fruit flies, suggested that natural selection "looked suspiciously like a tautology."

> "For, it may appear more than a truism," he wrote, "to state that the individuals that are the best adapted to survive have a better chance of surviving than those not so well adapted to survive." . . . the philosophical debate of the past ten to fifteen years has focused on precisely this point. The survival of the fittest? Any way of identifying the fittest other than by looking at the survivors? . . . Any way of identifying them other than by looking at the preserved ones? If not, then Darwin's theory is reduced from the status of scientific theory to that of tautology.[10]

Very quietly the Darwinians lost the debate and the theory of natural selection changed. "The admission that Darwin's theory of natural selection was tautological did not greatly bother the evolutionary theorists, however, because they had already taken the precaution of redefining natural selection to mean something quite different from what Darwin had in mind."[11] But, again, the general public was not told of the change — Darwinian theory remaine "a fact!"

British statistician and geneticist R. A. Fisher did the redefining of natural selection in his widely heralded book, *The Genetical Theory of Natural Selection*. Fisher made certain assumptions about birth and death rates and by combining them with Mendelian genetics he was able to qualify the resulting rates at which populations ratios changed. In 1976 C. H. Waddington, a prominent geneticist (who also spoke at the aforementioned Darwin Centennial in Chicago) said of Fisher's redefinition:

---

[10]*Ibid.*
[11]*Ibid.*, p. 74.

> The theory of neo-Darwinism is a theory of the evolution of the population in respect to leaving offspring and not in respect to anything.... Everybody has it in the back of his mind that the animals that leave the largest number of offspring are going to be those best adapted also for eating peculiar vegetation, or something of this sort, but this is not explicit in the theory.... There you do come to what is, in effect, a vacuous statement: Natural selection is that some things leave more offspring than others; and, you ask, which leave more offspring than others; and it is those that leave more offspring, and there is nothing more to it than that. *The whole real guts of evolution – which is how do you come to have horses and tigers and things – is outside the mathematical theory* [Bethell's emphasis].[12]

Darwin's theory was supposed to answer the question of how we got "horses and tigers and such." Yet, after several rather "secret" serious changes in the theory we are no closer to an answer (apart from God) than we were over 100 years ago!

I think we can see the point: Darwinism has *not* stood the test of time. There is a great deal of evidence for speciation (change within species) but none for the general theory of evolution – ameba to man. Yet, the debate goes on. *Harper's Magazine* (February 1985) had an excellent article by Tom Bethell entitled: "Agnostic Evolutionists: The Taxonomic Case Against Darwin," which I recommend to you. Bethell related that there are a growing number of agnostic scientists (not Christian scientists pushing creationism) who would be very happy if the theory of evolution just went away, because it does not help explain anything. Colin Patterson, an eminent scientist who published a pro-evolution book in 1978 entitled *Evolution*, published by the British Museum, now says, in reply to a creationist-activist:

> You say I should at least "show a photo of the fossil from which each type of organism was derived." I will lay it on the line – there is not one such fossil for which one could make a watertight argument. The reason is that statements about ancestry and descent are not applicable in the fossil record. Is *Archaeopteryx* the ancestor of all birds? Perhaps yes, perhaps

---

[12]*Ibid.*

no: there is no way of answering the question. It is easy enough to make up stories of how one form gave rise to another, and to find reasons why the stages should be favoured by natural selection. But such stories are not part of science, for there is no way of putting them to the test.[13]

Allow me one last quote from this article of Bethell's:

> Our belief, or "faith," that, as Patterson says, "all organisms have parents" ultimately derives from our acceptance of the philosophy of materialism. It is hard for us to understand (so long has materialism been the natural habitat of western thought) that this philosophy was not always accepted. In one of his essays on natural history reprinted in *Ever Since Darwin*, Steven Jay Gould suggests that Darwin delayed publishing his theory of evolution by natural selection because he was, perhaps unconsciously, waiting for the climate of materialism to become more firmly established. In his 1838 *M Notebook* Darwin wrote: "To avoid stating how far, I believe, in Materialism, say only that emotions, instincts, degrees of talent, which are hereditary are so because brain of child resembles parent stock." Darwin realized that the climate *had* changed — that evolution was "in the air" — in 1858 when he was jolted by Alfred Russell Wallace's paper outlining a theory of the mechanism of evolution very similar to his own.[14]

Some Clear Statements About the Issues

There is a real and important epistemological question as we have discussed in the section "The Nature and Definition of Science" as to what, in fact, constitutes "science." We seem to operate under the assumption that there are only two issues in the debate between science and religion: What has the status of "hypothesis," and what the status of "fact"? But there is a third issue more foundational than either of these: What is the philosophical framework of the discussion? It is clear that the scientist *qua* scientist has little to nothing to contribute to answering the ultimate question of origins.

The scientist can show that certain mechanisms do work or do not, in fact, work (for instance that the Lamarckian

---

[13]Tom Bethell, "Agnostic Evolutionists: The Taxonomic Case Against Darwin," *Harper's Magazine* February, 1985), p. 49.
[14]*Ibid.*, p. 61.

theory of genetic choice that Darwin used is wrong), but he cannot, as scientist, answer the historical question in regard to origins. Suppose Lamarck was right that one of these mechanisms for evolution does, in fact, work. What would it prove? That evolution was true? Certainly not. It would only prove that certain mechanisms work. Nothing else. It certainly would not answer the question of origins, nor prove it happened by that mechanism historically. The scientist *qua* scientist can tell us what does work now, given the current state of things.

What if a scientist, or much more likely, many scientists succeeded in creating life in a test tube. The old question! What would it prove about the question of origins? Nothing. If anything, it would indicate that it took extremely intelligent beings involved with very deliberate controlled conditions to create life. It certainly would not be supportive in any way of the theory of the chance coming into being of life as some seem to think.

I spoke in this appendix about the danger to Christian scientists of assuming the definitive truth of modern science, either via definition or methodology and reading an interpretation of modern science back into Scripture. But another *real* danger exists — that of a Christian scientist totally bifurcating his science from his faith stance. Science and Scripture must relate, as MacKay says. Truth is truth. Fact is fact. We must, as Christians, accept the challenge of John 8:32, for we must know the truth and the truth will set us free.

There are two very important questions in this discussion with regard to the theological nature of the issue which need to be addressed:

The first is the proper exegesis of Genesis 1-11. Allow me to say that we must not be so quick to "pontificate" on the meaning of Genesis 1-11 *without detailed exegesis*. It should be obvious that well educated Christians committed to the fundamentals of the faith and biblical inerrancy differ on the implications of such exegesis.

Whatever one's conclusions about what Genesis 1-11 teaches in regard to origins, we must realize that the question only really has interest and merit in the context of the question of the inspiration and authority of Scripture and biblical inerrancy.

Again, clearly what is at stake here is philosophical materialism, not the scientific data. What we need besides Christian scientists (and we do need Christian scientists) is Christian philosophers and philosophers of science. Christian scientists alone will not, cannot, answer the questions of origins. That will take Christian philosophers who are willing to pay the high academic price to be able to carry on credible world view construction and criticism.[15]

---

[15]For a bit more comprehensive discussion of some of the new developments between religion and science see part II of Miethe and Habermas, *Why Believe? God Exists! Rethinking the Case for God and Christianity*, Joplin: College Press, 1993.

D A Plea for the Practical Application of Christian Philosophy

Of all the academic disciplines taught in a college, university, or seminary, philosophy is quite often branded as the most famous (or infamous) of the so-called "ivory tower" subjects. In other words, philosophy is often selected as *the* area most characterized as scholars speaking to scholars with little relevance to the man on the street. Because it appears to be irrelevant and to have reached a "dead end," at least as practiced by some analytic philosophers, philosophy seems to suffer much from a lack of students who wish to major in this field. One important reason in this latter development is that philosophy is considered a very *impractical* preparation for life's work. While psychologists can counsel and make a good living by so doing, comparatively few can support a family by being practicing philosophers.

What makes philosophy so seemingly impractical as a profession for more than a select few? Or, why does philosophy appear to turn so many to skepticism when, by its nature, it should help people to see and understand that which *can* be known?

My concern is that I have witnessed too many good, but frustrated, students for whom philosophy became more of a hindrance than a help. I have seen too many budding young skeptics caused *by* the teaching of philosophy when this discipline should help *answer* the important questions of life.

The issue here is not whether philosophy should be taught — for in my estimation, it surely should be and should even be required. The critical issue is *how* it should be taught. It just might be that philosophy itself is not responsible for the harm but rather the incorrect teaching of it. Thus, I am surely not reacting to philosophy *per se* (since, at the very least, I would be cutting my own throat!) but to the current state of the teaching profession in this field. Self-criticism is very difficult, but easier than continually hearing sometimes valid criticism from those outside our field.

My purpose is one of critiquing current educational *methodologies* in the teaching of Christian philosophy and is not directly concerned with the *content* of the discipline, except in a few select instances. Accordingly, I purpose, first, to note briefly several methodological strengths and weaknesses involved in the teaching of philosophy, followed by some suggestions for the practical communication of philosophical concepts. A conclusion will attempt to tie these aspects together.

Methodological Weaknesses in Teaching Philosophy

In spite of the various individuals, institutions and philosophies involved, there do appear to be several pitfalls which are at least generally prevalent in the teaching of philosophy. Four of these will be briefly mentioned.

One apparent weakness is that this discipline often breeds pride both in the professor and the student. Too often, philosophy classes become an encouragement to one's ego. The unspoken creed recognized by many includes the call to debate at the drop of a hat, which often involves the belittling of the student in the name of providing an "example" of philosophy at work. After all, one is often tempted to ask, what would a fellow philosopher think if he saw me let this student off the hook after that stupid comment?

A critical point here is that such attitudes certainly rub off on students. This is perhaps nowhere more evident than when, after each "Introduction to Philosophy" class I teach, certain of my students become simply enamored with philosophy. However, a certain number of them seemingly define philosophy as the opportunity to showcase one's I.Q. level. I found it very amusing when one of my students used popular drag-racing jargon, saying that the purpose of philosophy is to teach one to "blow your opponents' doors off." This aptly describes the philosophical propensity to encourage pride.

Another problem is that, while philosophers should be students of the history of thought, we never seem to learn the error of countering one incorrect school of thought by advocating its exact reverse. In other words, we too often respond to one movement by encouraging the pendulum to swing too far in the opposite direction. Trends in philosophy verify this back-and-forth movement. In answer to Averroes' radical stress on reason, William of Occam had an almost equally radical stress on faith. In the Enlightenment, rationalism and empiricism were classically opposed, as each claimed a monopoly on truth (as if they were contradictory), while romanticism represented an overreaction to both. Yet another example is Kierkegaard's revolt against Hegelianism, both representing certain extremes, Even in the twentieth century, the current popularity of Eastern trends among certain scientists, philosophers and psychologists manifests itself as a backlash of mysticism against the last generations' positivism. Such overreactions are more than methodological, to be sure, but at least involve tendencies in this area that are to be avoided.

A third issue concerns a prevalent attitude among many, including evangelicals, that elevates either faith or the historical facts above its biblical importance. We affirm the equal importance of both the facts of the gospel and one's personal faith-commitment to them. Yet, we often devalue the one or the other in our philosophical methodology, sometimes leading to extreme positions that endanger the very nature of the gospel. To unduly elevate faith has led to various forms of the "leap of faith," while the over-elevation of reason often leads to various rationalistic errors.

The *former* mentality is often indicated by the fideistic distrust of virtually all use of reason or evidences. To ask questions or pursue apologetics is comparable to spiritual insubordination. The *latter* mentality sometimes manifests itself in the attitude that we need Catesian certainty, as if the evangelical answer to gaining scholarly recognition in academia is to be overly rational. The result is sometimes the downplaying of faith to a very menial level, that is, to what we do only after all of the evidence has been garnered.

Happily, these opposing attitudes in the faith-reason debate are not widespread in evangelicalism. But I fear they are still *too* common, and at least provide a very important area that demands our constant watchfulness. To be sure, while Paul was an accomplished apologist,[1] he offered numerous warnings even to Christians concerning the dangers of nonbiblical uses of reason.[2] So we, too, need to take note at this point.

A fourth problem concerns the current propensity of philosophers towards anti-epistemological teaching methods. Judging by the many "unofficial" experiences I have had both personally and heard reported by others in recent years, the secular philosophy class has too often become a time of tearing down all approaches to knowledge rather than building a positive case for what can be known to be true. Historically the "princes of epistemology," contemporary philosophy professors have sometimes exhibited a decided lack of interest in this area except by way of criticism. This has created a vacuum, because the job of constructing a viable world view has too often been abandoned by those whose chief job it is to build.

A caution here: This state of affairs is apparently much more common among non-Christian professors of philosophy than their Christian counterparts. And while the latter are perhaps guilty of "spoon-feeding" easy philosophical answers to their students on occasion, this essay by no means encourages such an approach. But giving sound grounds for what is knowable (or at least helping the student to narrow down some of the options) is certainly preferable to a methodology that attacks or questions all of a student's premises, as well as virtually all other plausible options, without replacing improper beliefs at all.

While such a methodology is apparently much less common with Christian professors of philosophy, this problem of anti-epistemology is not absent from evangelical circles. Thus, something we may not be guilty of personally needs our careful watchfulness nonetheless, lest we be guilty

---

[1] Acts 13-19 alone provides many valuable examples of apologetic argumentation by Paul. For some specific instances, see Acts 17:1-4, 22-34; 18:4.
[2] See 1 Cor. 1:19-31; 2:1-8; 2 Cor. 1:12; Col. 2:2-8 for examples.

of allowing our critiques to become a substitute for some foundation-laying, positive answers. I believe that philosophical defection at this point is one of the largest contributors to contemporary skepticism, which is both a dangerous legacy to give our students in the name of open-mindedness and a horrible methodology to have to answer for, since lives have been ruined in this manner. To both assist the student in working through the options and to give a valid basis for Christian belief is imperative in the practical teaching of Christian philosophy.

Methodological Strengths in Teaching Philosophy

Before making a number of practical suggestions for teaching Christian philosophy,[3] a few strengths of this discipline should be mentioned briefly, since these points have already been implied in the above section of this essay. For one like myself who is deeply committed to teaching philosophy and apologetics, the stating of these strengths is very important to the subject at hand.

One strength of philosophy is that it teaches students to *think* clearly and correctly. Christianity is increasingly seen, especially by unbelievers, as an irrational option, yet biblical belief offers a noteworthy corrective. The principles of logic and clear thinking are a needed remedy, applicable to everything from reading the daily newspaper to the study of intellectual theories. It by no means contradicts faith, but complements it. As even William Hordern recognized, "One cannot argue that fundamentalism is an irrational system."[4] As noted above, the facts and faith *must* work together. Our students must learn to think, but, of course, not at the expense of the above-mentioned problems.

Another benefit of Christian philosophy is that it is *the*

---

[3]By Christian philosophy (or Christian theism), I am chiefly referring to the general world view espoused by most evangelical Christians that minimally includes the gospel and both the philosophical and theological fundamental doctrines of the faith, although there will be many differences in nonessential areas.

[4]William B. Hordern. *A Layman's Guide to Protestant Theology* (New York; Macmillan Co., 1956). p. 68.

discipline best equipped to critique non-Christian philosophies. In a time of much proliferation of world views, we must not relinquish our task of pointing out various problems with views that fail on philosophical, historical, and biblical grounds. Our students must see the relevance of Christian philosophy at this point.

A third strength of Christian philosophy is to locate *new trends* in thought and to deal with them in a scholarly manner *before* they gain a strong foothold. Too often, we have been content to re-annihilate more-or-less defunct views such as logical positivism instead of launching out into new areas that definitely need our attention. Granted, it is easier to repeat old, clearly established points that are readily available in print. But we also need to exert some of our energies on new trends such as, for instance, the immense popularity today of combining Eastern thought and Western science, even among intellectuals. If we still devote all of our efforts to continuing to emphasize the demise of naturalism, we will fail to see the damage being done by this new movement, which often emphasizes a non-biblical return to many religious tenets.

As professors, we need to make our students aware of these new trends. We need to demonstrate that while Christian philosophy remains firm, our answers need to be flexible enough to be applied to new situations. Christian philosophy is certainly capable of handling such new confrontations, as Paul showed in the Book of Acts (see 17:2-4, 22-34). But we need to know *how* to make such applications ourselves, sometimes involving some creative apologetics, and how to communicate this ability to our students, lest we lose more ground to these new developments. Let us not wait until we are under heavy attack before we begin to move in this direction.

Lastly, if I might briefly indulge in a matter of content, a major strength of Christian philosophy is its stability and calling to build a positive world view. Not only do our students need to work through their own system, but they need to know *why* they believe *what* they believe. This may be the most important goal for us: to construct a system which, while perhaps differing in some methodological nonessentials from professor to professor, still expresses Christian tolerance to each other due to our agreement concerning the essentials. To build such a world view also involves the usage of apologetics in order to witness to the unbeliever by the power of the Holy Spirit, to strengthen the believer, and to pronounce our answers to the world *even if no one appears to be listening*.

These, then, are some of the strengths of Christian philosophy: to teach students to think clearly, be able to critique non-Christian world views, to locate and deal with new trends in thought and to construct a viable world view.

Because we so often miss the mark on methodological rather than theoretical grounds, I will now turn to some suggestions for the practical teaching of such Christian philosophy, some of which have already been mentioned explicitly and others that are implicitly present in the foregoing analysis.

Suggestions for the Practical Teaching of Philosophy

The following ten points will perhaps suggest a means of communicating philosophy in a biblical and practical, as well as theoretically correct, manner. It is not meant to be exhaustive, but is a modest proposal that we properly communicate the many truths of our discipline.

(1) We need to translate much of our Christian philosophy into *meaningful language*, especially at the undergraduate level, in particular. For those for whom "meaningfulness" is so important, why do we sometimes do such a poor job at *practical* meaningfulness? In the name of semantical purity, we often speak over students' heads so that they do not understand (as if semantical purity is more important than communication) and, more practically, we price ourselves out of some important marketplaces. It is *very* true that we need to teach philosophy correctly, including the use of proper terminology, but this is *not* synonymous with staying at such a level that we do not communicate. Both correct language and communication can occur. Professors of philosophy are still teachers and, as such, need to teach. We cannot "teach" without clear communication.

(2) We need to stress the *practical* side of philosophy. This can be done quite naturally, especially with lessons on more

practical topics, such as the applications of logic, the faith-reason issue, how philosophy can clear up some tough areas of theology, and with many current issues such as the popularity of Eastern thought. Here we can take advantage of the opportunity and carefully point out to students how philosophy can be practical, what options they have, as well as the repercussions of certain choices.

(3) We must be careful not to communicate false pride to our students; this comes naturally enough to all of us. We can be a negative example by haughtily acting as if philosophy is the "correct-all" to everything from faulty grammar to modern science, or by inferring that the answer to virtually any question is a debate complete with *ad hominen* "ripoffs," which then becomes a sort of "Christian street-fighting." We communicate this attitude clearly when we prefer to decimate our students rather than give them explanations. What we are actually teaching is, "Isn't it fun to have this type of knowledge and to be able to put people in their place?

Making ourselves look intelligent at the students' expense will usually produce several interested students who covet the same ability. We need to practice the Christian virtue of humility a bit more. It is easy to forget that when Peter commanded us to defend the faith, he also told us to do it "in meekness" (1 Pet. 3:15).

(4) We need to be careful that, in our own systems, we do not simply overreact to other world views, or that we do not overstress one side. What is a slight overstressing at present could easily become a massive gulf or a denial of important truth later at the hands of our students. I believe that we will have to give an account not only for our explicit teachings but also for our implicit errors.

As a colleague is fond of pointing out, truth is usually a very delicate balance between extremes. Some persons have a tendency to see only one side of a question, especially when they are exposed to it for the first time. The question for them might concern the identity of the latest author they have read. For instance, some are intrigued with skepticism when they are exposed to it. Yet, skepticism is no more correct (or even less so) than is a radically conservative philosophy that dogmatically claims to have all of the answers and all of the loose ends tied up. Again, philosophical truth is frequently a delicate balance of extreme views.

(5) As mentioned earlier, we must be ever so careful not to elevate reason so that faith suffers, or vice-versa. Personally, I have been more guilty of overstressing reason. Faith was always something very important, but too often its rightful place was ignored. Then I realized what was happening. Just because faith was important to me did not mean that it was balanced with reason. I had forgotten the dynamic, vibrant power of faith that, as C. S. Lewis noted, is our strongest means of trusting the facts over against the "blitzes" carried out by our changing moods.[5]

To suppress the biblical view of either faith or facts can also have an important affect on the gospel, the negative implications of which we would not want to communicate to any of our students. The elevation of the leap of faith has progressed to the very point of denying the facts of the gospel, while the elevation of reason and the need for Cartesian certainty leads to skepticism. To balance both facts and faith is to be both more biblical and more practical.

(6) We also need to make our *critiques* of other philosophical systems understandable in the sense that our students can communicate them successfully. In other words, these evaluations should not be so esoteric that, when confronted by such philosophies in everyday life, students have to respond by sending the person to their philosophy professor for details. It was quite rewarding when, on several separate occasions, the three of us in the philosophy departmentsaw some philosophy students do very well in one-on-one dialogues with more than a couple of nationally known non-Christian philosophers.

(7) We must teach our students how to detect and deal with new trends in thought. Often this can be taught quite popularly. I found that students responded well when asked, for instance, how they would react if confronted by a new

---

[5]C.S. Lewis, *Mere Christianity* (New York: Macmillan Co., 1952), pp. 122-124.

world view that admitted a basically supernatural outlook and hence Jesus' resurrection was seen as simply another so-called "miracle." This tendency is often part of the new Eastern view referred to earlier. I fear that we are sometimes so well-prepared for naturalistic options that we are not often ready for new departures. While our apologetics often remain the same, applications may differ radically. If we teach an apologetic system that is only one-dimensional, we may be poorly preparing our students.

(8) There is a real need today to *integrate* knowledge in various disciplines. We must show our students that philosophy is not an island unto itself, but a part of the knowledge which God has given to man. In particular, philosophy needs to be integrated with theology and other biblical truth. On a very simple level, it occurred to me one day that teaching in a private Christian college and not bringing a Bible to class along with my notes implied to my students, in some small way, that Christian philosophy can be pursued apart from God's revelation. We may scoff at this as being a bad example, but I believe that on occasion, students read us better than we do ourselves.

(9) We must be careful that our philosophy is *biblical.* Many of us have perhaps experienced the urge to first arrive at an initial philosophy, followed by a search for biblical "proof texts" that teach some vaguely similar thoughts. Our duty is to be sure that our world view is thoroughly Christian and biblical.

(10) Perhaps above all, we need to assist our students in positively building a Christian world view they can call their own. As mentioned earlier, this is a point of content as well as method. Spoon-feeding is not being advocated, as should be evident from my earlier comments. There is much room in many areas of philosophy for alternative viewpoints. But we can certainly provide a Christian "core" of essential fundamental beliefs. If we do not provide such positive input, skepticism could result and we will be avoiding what may be the most important task in Christian philosophy: to build a Christian world view for Christian living.

Conclusion

One person recently remarked to me, "I always thought of philosophy as two professors sitting around asking questions about what doesn't matter anyway." We have likely heard such comments numerous times and we need to hear them. However, philosophers usually dismiss such remarks with the feeling that we cannot expect the "uninitiated laity" to understand or appreciate our jargon. But if we were honestly evaluating our discipline, we might conclude that there are such impractical areas of philosophy and even in our teaching of it.

It is for this reason that this essay was prepared — as a plea to Christians, philosophers, and would-be philosophers to perform the calling to which God has called us in a much more biblical and practical manner. Whatever Paul meant by his numerous warnings against the unbiblical use of philosophy and reason, he *did* mean *something* about Christians misusing it, especially with regard to relying on man's wisdom rather than God's. We must be careful concerning all which this might entail.

One last and important warning is needed at this point. I have tried to be very careful not to imply in any way that philosophy is unimportant or that we need to sacrifice exactness in order to teach it. Otherwise I would be guilty of violating some of the tenets of this writing, both by giving easy answers to my students and by overreacting too far in the opposite direction. Rather I believe very strongly that philosophy and apologetics play a vital role in Christian education today and that what it has to offer is unique among the various academic disciplines. Thus, this is a plea to teach philosophy practically. Surely, if we believe that we have material of the utmost importance to present to our students, it is desireable to do so with a methodology that does not fail to get the message across properly. A balanced approach is called for — one that can both present the lofty truths of Christian philosophy, and do so meaningfully, practically and, above all, biblically.

—Gary R. Habermas, Ph.D.,
Honored Professor of Religion and Philosophy
at Emmanuel College, Oxford.

Select Bibliography

If this book has made clear to you the relationship between "faith" and "reason" — the inseparable tie between Christianity and knowledge; Christianity's claim to be wed to historical facts; and the great importance of our need to *continue learning* for effective knowledge of God, victory in Christian living, and meaningful evangelism — then you are not surprised to find this rather lengthy "select bibliography" here. This bibliography represents books covering the entire spectrum, from books for the beginner to those for the most advanced. You will not exhaust — outgrow — it, but you will find this bibliography food for building Christian maturity for a lifetime as you study the Scripture and read good literature to help you understand, support, and share your faith. It is not important where you are starting, but that you are starting to dig. May you grow steadily as you *dig deeply* into God's Word and the insight He has given men of thought! To help I have put a **"B"** after entries that a beginner will find better to start with and an **"I"** after those I consider especially important on whatever level they are written.

I. The Christian Mind:

Barclay, Oliver R. *The Intellect and Beyond: Developing a Christian Mind.* Grand Rapids, MI: Zondervan Publishing House, 1985. B

Blamires, Harry. *The Christian Mind.* London: S.P.C.K., 1963. I

Ferre, Nels F. S. *Faith and Reason.* New York: Harper & Brothers Publishers, 1946.

Gilson, Etienne. *Reason and Revelation in the Middle Ages.* New York: Charles Scribner's Sons, 1938.

Holmes, Arthur, Editor. *The Making of a Christian Mind: A Christian World View & the Academic Enterprise.* Downers Grove, IL: InterVarsity Press, 1985.

Miethe, Terry L. *The Christian's Guide to Faith & Reason*. Minneapolis, MN: Bethany House Publishers, 1987. B I

Stott, John R. W. *Your Mind Matters: The Place of the Mind in the Christian Life*. Downers Grove, IL: InterVarsity Press, 1972. B I

Woodbridge, John D., Editor. *Renewing Your Mind in a Secular World*. Chicago, IL: Moody Press, 1985.

Swinburne, Richard. *Faith and Reason*. Oxford, England: Clarendon Press, 1981.

Veith, Gene Edward Jr. *Loving God With All Your Mind: How to Survive and Prosper as a Christian In the Secular University and Post-Christian Culture*. Westchester, IL: Crossway Books, 1987. B I

II. Apologetics, General:

Bruce, Alexander B. *Apologetics; or, Christianity Defensively Stated*. New York: Charles Scribner's Sons, 1897.

Craig, William Lane. *Apologetics: An Introduction*. Chicago, IL: Moody Press, 1984. I

Dullas, Avery. *A History of Apologetics*. Grand Rapids, MI: Baker Book House, 1976.

Geisler, Norman L. *Christian Apologetics*. Grand Rapids, MI: Baker Book House, 1976. I

_____ . *False Gods of Our Time: A Defense of The Christian Faith*. Eugene, OR: Harvest House Publishers, 1985.

Gerstner, John H. *Reasons for Faith*. Grand Rapids, MI: Baker Book House, 1966. B

Green, Michael. *Runaway World*. Downers Grove, IL: InterVarsity Press, 1968. B I

Lewis, C. S. *Mere Christianity*. New York: Macmillan, 1960. I

Lewis, Gordon R. *Testing Christianity's Truth Claims: Approaches to Christian Apologetics*. Chicago, IL: Moody Press, 1976.

Little, Paul E. *Know Why You Believe*. Downers Grove, IL: InterVarsity Press, 1968. B

Macintosh, Douglas C. *The Reasonableness of Christianity*. New York: Scribner's Sons, 1926.

Miethe, Terry L. and Gary R. Habermas. *Why Believe? God Exists! Rethinking the Case for God and Christianity*. Joplin, MO: College Press Publishing, Inc., 1993. I

Montgomery, John Warwick. *Faith Founded on Fact: Essays in Evidential Apologetics*. Nashville, TN: Thomas Nelson Publishers, 1978.

Pinnock, Clark H. *Reason Enough: A Case for the Christian Faith.* Downers Grove, IL: InterVarsity Press, 1980.

_____. *Set Forth Your Case: An Examination of Christianity's Credentials.* Chicago, IL: Moody Press, 1971. I

Reid, J. K. S. *Christian Apologetics.* Grand Rapids, MI: Wm. B. Eerdmans, 1969.

Smith, Wilbur M. *Therefore Stand: A Plea for a Vigorous Apologetic in the Present Crisis of Evangelical Christianity.* Natick, MA: W. A. Wilde Co., 1945. I

Varghese, Roy A. *The Intellectuals Speak Out About God: A Handbook for the Christian Student in a Secular Society.* Chicago, IL: Regnery Gateway, 1984. I

III. Christian Evidences, General:

Little, Paul E. *Know Why You Believe.* Downers Grove, IL: InterVarsity Press, 1972. B

Gerstner, John H. *Reasons for Faith.* Grand Rapids, MI: Baker Book House, 1967. B

Hopkins, Mark. *Evidences of Christianity.* Boston, MA: T. R. Marvin & Son, 1909.

McDowell, Josh. *Evidence that Demands a Verdict: Historical Evidences for the Christian Faith.* San Bernardino, CA: Campus Crusade for Christ International, 1972. B

Ramm, Bernard. *Protestant Christian Evidences: A Textbook of the Evidences of the Truthfulness of the Christian Faith for Conservative Protestants.* Chicago, IL: Moody Press, 1953.

Row, C. A. *A Manual of Christian Evidences.* London: Hodder and Stoughton, 1907.

IV. Christian Philosophy, General:

Brown, Colin. *Philosophy and the Christian Faith: A Historical Sketch from the Middle Ages to the Present Day.* Downers Grove, IL: InterVarsity Press, 1969.

Geisler, Norman L. *Philosophy of Religion.* Grand Rapids, MI: Zondervan Publishing House, 1974. I

_____, and Paul D. Feinberg. *Introduction to Philosophy: A Christian Perspective.* Grand Rapids, MI: Moody Press, 1980. B

Holmes, Arthur F. *Christian Philosophy in the 20th Century: An Essay in Philosophical Methodology.* Nutley, NJ: The Craig Press, 1969.

_____. *Philosophy: A Christian Perspective, An Introductory Essay.* Downers Grove, IL: 1975. B I

Langmead-Casserley, J. V. *The Christian in Philosophy*. London: Faber and Faber, 1949.

Lynch, Lawrence E. *A Christian Philosophy*. New York: Charles Scribner's Sons, 1968.

Maritain, Jacques. *The Degrees of Knowledge*. New York: Charles Scribner's Sons, 1938.

Nash, Ronald H. *Faith & Reason: Searching for a Rational Faith*. Grand Rapids, MI: Zondervan, 1988. I

_____ . *An Introduction to Philosophy*. London: Sheed and Ward, 1930.

Thompson, Samuel M. *A Modern Philosophy of Religion*. Chicago, IL: Henry Regnery Co., 1955. I

Trueblood, David Elton. *Philosophy of Religion*. New York: Harper and Row, 1957.

Young, Warren C. *A Christian Approach to Philosophy*. Grand Rapids, MI: Baker Book House, 1954.

V. Christian Theology, General:

Bloesch, Donald. *Essentials of Evangelical Theology*. 2 Volumes. San Francisco: Harper & Row, 1978-1979.

Calvin, John. *Institutes of the Christian Religion*. 2 Volumes. Edited by J. T. McNeill. *Library of Christian Classics*. Philadelphia: Westminster, 1960.

Campbell, Alexander. *The Christian System*. Nashville, TN: Gospel Advocate Co., 1956. I

Erickson, Millard J. *Christian Theology*. 3 Volumes. Grand Rapids: Baker, 1983-1986.

Finney, Charles G. *Finney's Systematic Theology*. Minneapolis: Bethany House Publishers, 1976.

Henry, Carl F. H. *God, Revelation and Authority*. 5 Volumes. Waco, TX: Word Books, 1976-1983. I

Pieper, Franz. *Christian Dogmatics*. 4 Volumes. St. Louis: Concordia, 1950-1957.

Pinnock, Clark H. (Editor) *The Grace of God, The Will of Man*. Grand Rapids, MI: Zondervan, 1989. I

_____ , Editor. *Grace Unlimited*. Minneapolis, MN: Bethany House Publishers, 1975.

Milligan, Robert. *The Scheme of Redemption*. Nashville, TN: Gospel Advocate Co., 1869.

VI. Christian Theism:

Balfour, A. J. *The Foundations of Belief.* New York: Longmans, Green, and Co., 1895.

_____ . *Theism and Humanism.* New York: George H. Doran Co., 1915.

_____ . *Theism and Thought.* London: Hodder and Stoughton, 1923.

Hackett, Stuart C. *The Resurrection of Theism: Prolegomena to Christian Apology.* Second Edition. Grand Rapids, MI: Baker Book House, 1982. I

Orr, James. *The Christian View of God and the World.* Edinburgh: Andrew Elliot, 1902.

Purtill, Richard L. *Reason to Believe.* Grand Rapids, MI: Wm. B. Eerdmans, 1974.

Swinburne, Richard. *The Coherence of Theism.* Oxford, England: Clarendon Press, 1977. I

VII. The Existence of God:

Adler, Mortimer J. *How to Think About God: A Guide for the 20th-Century Pagan.* New York: Collier Books, Macmillan Publishing Co., 1980.

Burrill, Donald R., Editor. *The Cosmological Arguments: A Spectrum of Opinion.* Garden City, N.Y: Doubleday & Co., Inc., 1967.

Collins, James. *God in Modern Philosophy.* Chicago, IL: Henry Regnery Co., 1959.

Craig, William Lane. *The Existence of God and the Beginning of the Universe.* San Bernardino, CA: Here's Life Publishers, Inc., 1979. B

Garrigou-Lagrange, R. *God: His Existence and His Nature, A Thomistic Solution of Certain Agnostic Antinomies.* Vol. I. St. Louis, MO., B. Herder Book Co., 1934.

Gilson, Etienne. *God and Philosophy.* New Haven, CT: Yale University Press, 1941.

Hartshorne, Charles. *Anselm's Discovery: A Re-examination of the Ontological Proof for God's Existence.* LaSalle, IL: Open Court Publishing Co., 1965.

_____ . *Creative Synthesis and Philosophic Method.* LaSalle, IL: Open Court Publishing Co., 1970.

_____ , and William L. Reese, Editors. *Philosophers Speak of God.* Chicago, IL: The University of Chicago Press, 1953.

Kung, Hans. *Does God Exist? An Answer for Today*. Garden City, N.Y: Doubleday & Co., Inc., 1980.

Miethe, Terry L. and Antony G.N. Flew. *Does God Exist? A Believer and an Atheist Debate*. San Francisco, CA: Harper Collins, 1991. I

Plantinga, Alvin. *God and Other Minds: A Study of the Rational Justification of Belief in God*. Ithaca, N.Y: Cornell University Press, 1967.

_____ , Editor. *The Ontological Argument: From St. Anselm to Contemporary Philosophers*. Garden City, N.Y: Doubleday & Co. Inc., 1965.

Reichenbach, Bruce R. *The Cosmological Argument: A Reassessment*. Springfield, IL: Charles C. Thomas Publisher, 1972. I

Swinburne, Richard. *The Existence of God*. Oxford, England: Clarendon Press, 1979.

VIII. The Deity of Christ:

Buell, Jon A., and O. Quentin Hyder. *Jesus: God, Ghost or Guru?* Grand Rapids, MI: Zondervan Publishing House, 1978. B I

Geisler, Norman L. *Christ: The Theme of the Bible*. Chicago, IL: Moody Press, 1968. B

Liddon, Henry Parry. *The Divinity of Our Lord*. London: Pickering and Inglis, 1866.

Mackintosh, H. R. *The Doctrine of the Person of Jesus Christ*. New York: Charles Scribner's Sons, 1931. I

Morris, Leon. *The Lord From Heaven*. London: InterVarsity Press, 1958.

Smith, Wilbur M. *The Supernaturalness of Christ: Can We Still Believe in It?* Boston: W. A. Wilde Co., 1954. I

Warfield, Benjamin B. *The Lord of Glory: A Study of the Designations of Our Lord in the New Testament with Especial Reference to His Deity*. London: Hodder and Stoughton, 1907. I

IX. The Virgin Birth:

Hanke, Howard A. *The Validity of the Virgin Birth*. Grand Rapids: Zondervan Publishing House, 1963.

Machen, J. Gresham. *The Virgin Birth of Christ*. New York: Harper and Row, 1930.

Orr, James. *The Virgin Birth of Christ*. New York: Charles Scribner's Sons, 1907. I

X. The Resurrection:

Craig, William Lane. *The Son Rises: Historical Evidence for the Resurrection of Jesus*. Chicago, IL: Moody Press, 1981. B

Durrwell, F. X. *The Resurrection: A Biblical Study*. New York: Sheed & Ward, 1960. I

Green, Michael. *Man Alive!* Downers Grove, IL: InterVarsity Press, 1967. B I

_____ . *The Empty Cross of Jesus*. Downers Grove, IL: InterVarsity Press, 1984.

Habermas, Gary R. *The Resurrection of Jesus: A Rational Inquiry*. Ann Harbor, MI: University Microfilms, 1976.

_____ . *The Resurrection of Jesus: An Apologetic*. Grand Rapids, MI: Baker Book House, 1980. B

_____ . *Ancient Evidence for the Life of Jesus: Historical Records of His Death and Resurrection*. Nashville, TN: Thomas Nelson Publishers, 1984. I

Kunneth, Walter. *The Theology of the Resurrection*. St. Louis, MO: Concordia Publishing House, 1965. I

Ladd, George E. *I Believe in the Resurrection of Jesus*. Grand Rapids, MI: Wm. B. Eerdmans, 1975.

Miethe, Terry L. (Editor), Gary R. Habermas and Antony G. N. Flew. *Did Jesus Rise from the Dead? The Resurrection Debate*. San Francisco, CA: Harper & Row, 1987. I

Orr, James. *The Resurrection of Jesus*. Grand Rapids, MI: Zondervan Publishing House, 1965. I

Pannenburg, Wolfhart. *Jesus – God and Man*. Philadelphia, PA: The Westminster Press, 1968.

Ramsey, A. M. *The Resurrection of Christ*. London: Geoffrey Bless, 1962. B

Sparrow-Simpson, W. J. *Our Lord's Resurrection*. Grand Rapids, MI: Zondervan Publishing House, 1964.

_____ . *The Resurrection and the Christian Faith*. Grand Rapids, MI: Zondervan Publishing House, 1968.

Tenney, Merrill C. *The Reality of the Resurrection*. New York: Harper & Row, 1963. B

_____ . *The Vital Heart of Christianity*. Grand Rapids, MI: Zondervan Publishing House, 1964. B I

Wenham, John. *Easter Enigma: Are the Resurrection Accounts in Conflict?* Grand Rapids, MI: Zondervan Publishing House, 1984. B

XI. Miracles:

Best, John H. *The Miracles of Christ: In the Light of Our Present-Day Knowledge.* London: S. P. C. K., 1937.

Bruce, Alexander B. *The Miraculous Element in the Gospels.* London: Hodder and Stoughton, 1886.

Geisler Norman L. *Miracles and Modern Thought.* Grand Rapids, MI: Zondervan Publishing House, 1982. I

Lewis, C. S. *Miracles: How God Intervenes in Nature and Human Affairs.* New York: Macmillian Publishing Co., 1947. I

Swinburne, Richard. *The Concept of Miracle.* London: Macmillan Publishing Co., 1970.

Taylor, William M. *The Miracles of Our Saviour.* London: Hodder and Stoughton, 1891.

Trench, Richard C. *Notes on the Miracles of Our Lord.* London: Pickering and Inglis, 1953.

Warfield, Benjamin B. *Miracles: Yesterday and Today, True and False.* Grand Rapids, MI: Wm. B. Eerdmans, 1918.

XII. The Bible, General:

Archer, Gleason L. *Encyclopedia of Bible Difficulties.* Grand Rapids, MI: Zondervan Publishing House, 1982. I

_____. *A Survey of Old Testament Introduction.* Chicago, IL: Moody Press, 1964. I

Barker, Glenn W., William L. Lane, and J. Ramsey Michaels. *The New Testament Speaks.* New York: Harper & Row, 1969. I

Bruce, F. F. *The Christian Approach to the Old Testament.* London: InterVarsity Press, 1955. B

_____. *The Defense of the Gospel in the New Testament.* Grand Rapids, MI: Wm. B. Eerdmans, 1977. B

_____. *New Testament Development of Old Testament Themes.* Grand Rapids, MI: Wm. B. Eerdmans, 1968. B

_____. *The New Testament Documents: Are They Reliable?* Grand Rapids, MI: Wm. B. Eerdmans, 1953. B I

_____. *The Message of the New Testament.* Grand Rapids, MI: Wm. B. Eerdmans, 1972. B

Danker, Frederick W. *Multipurpose Tools for Bible Study.* Second Revised Edition. St. Louis: Concordia Publishing House, 1966.

Douglas, James D., Editor. *The New Bible Dictionary.* Grand Rapids: Wm. B. Eerdmans, 1962.

Geisler, Norman L. *Decide for Yourself: How History Views the Bible.* Grand Rapids, MI: Zondervan Publishing House, 1982.

_____ , and William E. Nix. *A General Introduction to the Bible.* Chicago, IL: Moody Press, 1968. B I

Harrington, D. J. *The New Testament: A Bibliography.* Wilmington, DE: Michael Glazier, Inc., 1985.

XIII. How We Got Our Bible:

Bruce, F. F. *The Books and the Parchments.* Westwood, NJ: Fleming H. Revell Co., 1963. I

_____ . *The Canon of Scripture.* Downers Grove, IL: InterVarsity Press, 1988. I

_____ . *The English Bible: A History of Translations from the Earliest English Versions to the New English Bible.* Oxford, England: Oxford University Press, 1970. I

Carson, D. A. *The King James Version Debate: A Plea for Realism.* Grand Rapids, MI: Baker Book House, 1979.

Goodspeed, Edgar J. *How Came The Bible?* Nashville, TN: Abingdon Press, 1940.

Harris, R. Laird. *Inspiration and Canonicity of the Bible.* Grand Rapids, MI: Zondervan Publishing House, 1957. I

Lightfoot, Neil R. *How We Got the Bible.* Grand Rapids, MI: Baker Book House, 1964.

Westcott, B. F. *A General Survey of the History of the Canon of the New Testament.* New York: Macmillian and Co., 1889. I

XIV. Inspiration of the Bible:

Bruce, F. F. *The New Testament Documents: Are They Reliable?* Grand Rapids, MI: Wm. B. Eerdmans, 1960. B I

Henry, Carl F. H., Editor. *Revelation and the Bible: Contemporary Evangelical Thought.* Grand Rapids, MI: Baker Book House, 1958.

Hodge, Archibald A., and Benjamin B. Warfield. *Inspiration.* Grand Rapids, MI: Baker Book House, 1979.

Orr, James. *Revelation and Inspiration.* Grand Rapids, MI: Wm. B. Eerdmans, 1952.

Packer, James I. *God Speaks to Man: Revelation and the Bible.* Philadelphia, PA: Westminster Press, 1966. I

Pinnock, Clark H. *Biblical Revelation: The Foundation of Christian Theology.* Chicago, IL: Moody Press, 1971. I

_____ . *A Defense of Biblical Infallibility.* Philadelphia, PA: Presbyterian and Reformed Publishing Co., 1967. B I

_____ . *The Scripture Principle.* San Francisco, CA: Harper & Row, 1984.

Warfield, Benjamin B. *The Inspiration and Authority of the Bible.* Philadelphia: Presbyterian and Reformed Publishing Co., 1958. I

XV. Biblical Inerrancy:

Carson, D. A., and John D. Woodbridge., Editors. *Scripture and Truth.* Grand Rapids, MI: Zondervan Publishing Co., 1983.

Custer, Stewart. *Does Inspiration Demand Inerrancy?* Nutley, NJ: Craig Press, 1968.

Geisler, Norman L., Editor. *Biblical Errancy: An Analysis of its Philosophical Roots.* Grand Rapids, MI: Zondervan Publishing House, 1981. I

_____ , Editor. *Inerrancy.* Grand Rapids, MI: Zondervan Publishing House, 1979.

Gerstner, John H. *Bible Inerrancy Primer.* Grand Rapids, MI: Baker Book House, 1965. B

Lewis, Gordon., and Bruce Demarest., Editors. *Challenges to Inerrancy: A Theological Response.* Chicago, IL: Moody Press, 1984.

Montgomery, John Warwick., Editor. *God's Inerrant Word: An International Symposium of the Trustworthiness of Scripture.* Minneapolis, MN: Bethany Fellowship, Inc., 1974.

Youngblood, Ronald., Editor. *Evangelicals and Inerrancy: Selections from the Journal of the Evangelical Theological Society.* Nashville, TN: Thomas Nelson Publishers, 1984.

XVI. The Bible and Archaeology:

Bruce, F. F. *Second Thoughts on the Dead Sea Scrolls.* Grand Rapids, MI: Wm. B. Eerdmans, 1959.

Burroughs, Miller. *What Mean These Stones?* New Haven, CT: American Schools of Oriental Research, 1941.

Free, Joseph P. *Archaeology and Bible History.* Wheaton, IL: Scripture Press, 1964. I

Kenyon, Frederick G. *The Bible and Archaeology.* New York: Harper and Brothers, 1940.

Lewis, Jack P. *Historical Backgrounds of Bible History.* Grand Rapids, MI: Baker Book House, 1971. B

Owen, George F. *Archaeology and the Bible.* Westwood, NJ: Fleming H. Revell Co., 1961. B

Unger, Merrill F. *Archaeology and the Old Testament.* Grand Rapids, MI: Zondervan Publishing House, 1966. I

———. *Archaeology and the New Testament*. Grand Rapids, MI: Zondervan Publishing House, 1962.

XVII. Fulfilled Prophecy:

Payne, J. Barton. *Encyclopedia of Biblical Prophecy: The Complete Guide to Scriptural Predictions and Their Fulfillment*. San Francisco, CA: Harper & Row, 1973. I

XVIII. The Problem of Evil:

Geisler, Norman L. *Philosophy of Religion*. "Part Four — God and Evil." Grand Rapids, MI: Zondervan Publishing House, 1974. I

———. *The Roots of Evil*. Grand Rapids, MI: Zondervan Publishing House, 1978.

Lewis, C. S. *The Problem of Pain*. New York: Macmillan Co., 1962. I

Wenham, John W. *The Goodness of God*. Downers Grove, IL: InterVarsity Press, 1974. I

XIX. Bible and Science:

Clark, Robert E. D. *Darwin: Before and After*. Chicago, IL: Moody Press, 1967. B

Clark, Robert T., and James D. Bales. *Why Scientists Accept Evolution*. Grand Rapids, MI: Baker Book House, 1966.

Clark, Gordon H. *The Philosophy of Science and Belief in God*. Nutley, NJ: Craig Press, 1964. I

Gange, Robert. *Origins and Destiny*. Waco, TX: Word Books, 1986. I

Gish, Duane T. *Evolution: The Fossils Say No!* San Diego: Institute for Creation Research, 1972.

Hayward, Alan. *God's Truth! A Scientist Shows Why it Makes Sense to Believe the Bible*. Nashville, TN: Thomas Nelson Publishers, 1983. B

Hummel Charles E. *The Galileo Connection: Resolving Conflicts between Science & the Bible*. Downers Grove, IL: InterVarsity Press, 1986.

Klotz, John W. *Genes, Genesis and Evolution*. St. Louis, MO: Concordia Publishing House, 1970. I

MacBeth, Norman. *Darwin Retried: An Appeal to Reason*. Ipswich, MA: Gambit, 1971. I

MacKay, Donald M. *Science and the Quest for Meaning*. Grand Rapids, MI: Wm. B. Eerdmans, 1982. B I

Morris, Henry M. *Evolution and the Modern Christian*. Grand Rapids, MI: Baker Book House, 1967.

_____. *The Twilight of Evolution*. Grand Rapids, MI: Baker Book House, 1963.

_____, and Gary E. Parker. *What is Creation Science?* San Diego, CA: Creation-Life Publishers, Inc., 1982. B

Thaxton, Charles B., Walter L. Bradley, and Roger L. Olson. *The Mystery of Life's Origin: Reassessing Current Theories*. New York: Philosophical Library, 1984. I

Whitcomb, John C., and Henry M. Morris. *The Genesis Flood: The Biblical Record and Its Scientific Implications*. Grand Rapids, MI: Baker Book House, 1970.

Wilder-Smith, A. E. *Creation of Life*. Wheaton, IL: Harold Shaw Publishers, 1970. I

_____. *He Who Thinks Has to Believe*. Costa Mesa, CA: TWFT, 1981. B

_____. *Man's Origin, Man's Destiny*. Minneapolis, MN: Bethany House Publishers, 1968. I

_____. *The Natural Sciences Know Nothing of Evolution*. Costa Mesa, CA: TWFT Publishers, 1981. I

_____. *The Scientific Alternative to Neo-Darwinian Evolutionary Theory: Information Sources and Structures*. Costa Mesa, CA: TWFT Publishers, 1987. I

XX. Evangelism and Missions:

Aldrich, Joseph C. *Life-Style Evangelism: Crossing Traditional Boundaries to Reach the Unbelieving World*. Portland, OR: Multnomah Press, 1981. B I

Coleman, Robert E. *The Master Plan of Evangelism*. Old Tappan, NJ: Fleming H. Revell Co., 1963. I

Eims, Leroy. *The Lost Art of Disciple Making*. Colorado Springs, CO: Navpress and Zondervan Publishing House, 1978.

Green, Michael. *Evangelism in the Early Church*. Grand Rapids, MI: Wm. B. Eerdmans, 1970.

_____. *Evangelism Now and Then*. Downers Grove, IL: InterVarsity Press, 1979.

Petersen, Jim. *Evangelism for Our Generation*. Colorado Springs, CO: Navpress, 1985.

XXI. Discipleship and Christian Living:

Bonhoeffer, Dietrich. *The Cost of Discipleship*. New York: Macmillan, 1969. I

Collins, Gary R. *Beyond Easy Believism.* Waco, TX: Word Books, 1982.

Discipleship Journal. Published bimonthly by The Navigators, 3820 North Thirtieth Street, Colorado Springs, Colorado. New subscriptions write: *Discipleship Journal,* Subscription Services, Post Office Box 1113, Dover, New Jersey 07801. This is an excellent resource with many good articles per issue!

Friesen, Garry. *Decision Making & The Will of God: A Biblical Alternative to the Traditional View.* Portland, OR: Multnomah Press, 1980. I

Hansel, Tim. *When I Relax I Feel Guilty.* Elgin, IL: David C. Cook Publishing Co., 1979.

MacDonald, Gordon. *Ordering Your Private World.* Nashville, TN: Oliver Nelson, 1984.

McDonald, William. *True Discipleship.* Kansas City, MO: Walterick Publishers, 1962.

Miethe, Terry L. *The New Christian's Guide to Following Jesus.* Minneapolis, MN: Bethany House Publishers, 1984. B I

Mitchell, C. C. *Let's Live: Christ in Everyday Life.* Old Tappan, NJ: Fleming H. Revell Co., 1975. B

Murray, Andrew. *Believer's Absolute Surrender.* In the "Andrew Murry Christian Maturity Library," Minneapolis, MN: Bethany House Publishers, Inc., 1985. B I

Schaeffer, Francis A. *The Mark of a Christian.* Downers Grove, IL: InterVarsity Press, 1970. B

_____. *True Spirituality.* Wheaton, IL: Tyndale House Publishers, 1971.

Stott, John R. W. *Basic Christianity.* Downers Grove, IL: InterVarsity Press, 1972. B

XXII. Christianity and History:

Brown, Colin, Editor. *History, Criticism and Faith.* Downers Grove, IL: InterVarsity Press, 1976.

Ferguson, Everett. *Backgrounds of Early Christianity.* Grand Rapids, MI: Baker, 1987.

Fischer, David Hackett. *Historians' Fallacies: Toward a Logic of Historical Thought.* New York: Harper & Row, 1970. I

Marsden, George, and Frank Roberts, Editors. *A Christian View of History?* Grand Rapids, MI: Wm. B. Eerdmans, 1975.

Montgomery, John W. *History and Christianity.* Downers Grove, IL: InterVarsity Press, 1965. B

_____ . *The Shape of the Past: An Introduction to Philosophical Historiography*. Minneapolis, MN: Bethany House Publishers, 1962.

_____ . *Where is History Going?* Minneapolis, MN: Bethany House Publishers, 1969.

Nash, Ronald H. *Christian Faith & Historical Understanding*. Grand Rapids, MI: Zondervan Publishing House, 1984.

Woodbridge, John D. *Great Leaders of the Christian Church*. Chicago, IL: Moody Press, 1988. B I

XXIII. The Christian and the University:

Newman, John Henry. *The Idea of a University Defined and Illustrated*. London: Longman's Green, and Co., 1893. I

Malik, Charles H. *A Christian Critique of the University*. Downers Grove, IL: InterVarsity Press, 1982. B

Ong, Walter J., Editor. *Knowledge and the Future of Man*. New York: Simon and Schuster, 1968.

Whitehead, Alfred North. *The Aims of Education*. New York: Mentor Books, The New American Library, 1949. I

XXIV. Reference Works:

Douglas, J.D. (General Editor). *The New International Dictionary of the Christian Church*. Revised Edition. Grand Rapids, MI: Zondervan, 1978. I

_____ ; F. F. Bruce; J. I. Packer; N. Hillyer; D. Guthrie; A. R. Millard; D. J. Wiseman (Eds.) *New Bible Dictionary*. Second Edition. Wheaton, IL: Tyndale House Publishers, Inc., 1982. I

Ferguson, Everett (Ed.) *Encyclopedia of Early Christianity*. New York: Garland, 1992.

Ferguson, Sinclair B.; David F. Wright; and J. I. Packer (Eds). *New Dictionary of Theology*. Downers Grove, IL: InterVarsity Press, 1988. I

Miethe, Terry L. *The Compact Dictionary of Doctrinal Words*. Minneapolis, MN: Bethany House Publishers, 1988. B

Unger, Merrill F. *The New Unger's Bible Dictionary*. R. K. Harrison, Editor; Howard F. Vos and Cyril J. Barber, Contributing Editors. Chicago: Moody Press, 1988.

_____ . *The New Unger's Bible Handbook*. Revised by Gary N. Larson. Chicago: Moody Press, 1984.